P2D

Elements of a Growth Mindset

TABATHA TURMAN

Archway Publishing books may be ordered through booksellers or by contacting:

Archway Publishing
1663 Liberty Drive
Bloomington, IN 47403
www.archwaypublishing.com
844-669-3957

Because of the dynamic nature of the Internet, any web addresses or
links contained in this book may have changed since publication and
may no longer be valid. The views expressed in this work are solely those
of the author and do not necessarily reflect the views of the publisher,
and the publisher hereby disclaims any responsibility for them.

Any people depicted in stock imagery provided by Getty Images are
models, and such images are being used for illustrative purposes only.
Certain stock imagery © Getty Images.

Interior Graphics/Art Credit: Tabatha Turman

ISBN: 978-1-6657-2913-0 (sc)
ISBN: 978-1-6657-2912-3 (hc)
ISBN: 978-1-6657-2911-6 (e)

Library of Congress Control Number: 2022916055

Print information available on the last page.

Archway Publishing rev. date: 11/30/2022

DEDICATION

To my mother, who taught me to be resilient and persevere regardless of the hand I've been dealt, and to my two sons, who amaze me with their will and drive to live a life true to their passions and dreams.

Dear Andrea,

Hopefully you find valuable gems as you read P2b

HAPPY READING!!.

Be Encouraged,

CONTENTS

Introduction ix

Chapter 1   Discover Your P²D 1
Chapter 2   Choices and Channeling 12
Chapter 3   Build Your Brand 31
Chapter 4   Build a Network 48
Chapter 5   Be Intentional 65
Chapter 6   Use Your Fear as Fuel 86
Chapter 7   Find Your Higher Purpose 106
Chapter 8   Develop a Growth Mindset 121
Chapter 9   Claim Your Destiny 135

INTRODUCTION

I always knew as a little girl that I would serve in leadership or own a business one day. I could not articulate it as clearly back then. However, there were signs early on.

The purpose of this book is to allow you to take a journey backward, self-reflecting on circumstances and situations that have shaped you as the leader you are today and what ignites your passion purpose drive (P2D). It will also show you how to use the tools in your life toolkit to course correct or enhance your leadership style and goals. The earlier you start to assess your toolkit, the earlier you can learn about the possibilities as discussed in chapter 1, "Discover Your P²D."

In elementary school, I participated in Junior Achievement. This was an organization that brought businesspeople and entrepreneurs into the community to speak with us about their professions. It was very interesting and intriguing to me. The people who came were in professions that we did not have access to in my municipality of Pine Lawn, a city located in St. Louis, Missouri. The entrepreneurial seed was planted at a very early age, and I couldn't stop dreaming about starting a business.

When I speak to young people, I always emphasize that formal education gave me a couple of degrees and some knowledge while the informal education that I received as a young girl in St. Louis, Missouri, opened my eyes, ignited my passion, intensified my curiosity, and gave me the perseverance and drive to grow as a leader and one day start my business Integrated Finance and Accounting Solutions (IFAS).

Once I reached high school, I joined Future Business Leaders of America (FBLA) and Distributive Education Clubs of America

(DECA). Both organizations were designed to teach students about marketing their products and services as a businessperson working at a company or as an entrepreneur. In FBLA, we would compete against other schools to market our fictitious products and services to judges. I remember being overjoyed when my picture appeared in the local newspaper participating in a competition.

DECA prepares emerging leaders and entrepreneurs for careers in marketing, finance, hospitality, and management in high schools and colleges around the globe. My teacher at Jennings Senior High School, who served as the advisor for both groups, ran a family-owned shoe store in her hometown. Her stories of growing up working in the business and second-generation challenges always had me on the edge of my seat. She was also my cheerleading coach. Whenever she talked about her business, I remember once again becoming intrigued.

Membership in these organizations nurtured the seed that had already been planted during my Junior Achievement days. I couldn't articulate it at the time, but now I know that FBLA and DECA were social networks to surround myself with like-minded teens in business and entrepreneurship. My P²D started to come to life without me knowing it.

Throughout my leadership journey in the military and business, every assignment that I was given was all part of the journey to nurturing my P²D. I could never understand why I got the jobs in the military that kept me at work sixteen hours a day and away from my family from six to twelve months at a time. I would always say that in the next chapter of my life, I will be working for myself. I can give these sixteen- to eighteen-hour days to my company.

As my time on active duty came to an end, I began researching various franchises. I received franchise information from Subway, H&R Block, McDonald's, Cookie Bouquet, and Candy Bouquet. I was not led to follow any of those business models because of a lack of resources or interest. However, I still had a need to nurture that seed planted in my early years.

I am a glass-half-full type of person, so as I learned lessons from the battlefield to use in business and life, it got me to where I needed to be. My last assignment on active duty from 2004 to 2005 as a finance detachment commander in Iraq was my toughest. Little did I know that one day the experience I gained from this assignment would help me at IFAS in managing forward-deployed employees in Iraq, Afghanistan, and Kuwait. I could manage the project operations on the ground without physically being there based on past experiences serving in Iraq.

Let's fast-forward to today. As of January 2022, I have been in business for fifteen years. I am confident that most, if not all, of the triumphs and failures over the years were to teach me that there are rewards and consequences associated with life's choices as discussed in chapter 2, "Make Choices, Channel Your P²D."

How can we continue to live out our P²D rather than play it safe? We must take lessons as an opportunity to learn and grow. We must never lose sight of what we were destined to be by taking a self-inventory of the common threads that run through the experiences in our lives. It is important to understand how you constantly show up. If it is contrary to the leadership or company brand that you are building, how do you change people's perception? Chapter 3, "Build Your Brand," will guide you closer to that self-discovery.

While building a brand, who you associate with and how you spend your time are very important, as discussed in chapter 4, "Build a Network," and chapter 5, "Be Intentional." As mentioned earlier, in high school in DECA and FBLA, my little network of like-minded individuals was starting to form. In these safe spaces built with intention, I was allowed to share dreams and visions and be held accountable without the fear of being laughed at for dreaming outside of the norm at the time.

For some of us, negative thoughts and the inability to move

forward when trying to accomplish goals can be attributed to what someone has said we couldn't do. In most cases, to actualize our P²D, we have to consciously isolate family influences and traits. What did your mother tell you? What effect do your siblings have on you? Past experiences of what people have told us sometimes become the whispering voice of the parrot on the shoulder, repeating those things that caused you to feel fear, self-defeated, and unequipped to become the person that you visualize or see in the mirror.

In chapter 6, "Use Your Fear as Fuel," you will learn how other leaders kept their P²D burning brightly, defying societal and familial norms and the whispers of the parrot on the shoulder.

As I continued to use my past experiences to learn and grow, community consciousness was woven into the ethos of my corporate culture. As a leader, you must be concerned about the welfare of other people. A sense of empowerment comes from putting creative thoughts together to help your community grow, leaving it better for the next generation. We are all unique, and there is no one else in the world like you and what you tie your higher purpose to, as discussed in chapter 7, "Find Your Higher Purpose."

I truly believe that once you realize your full potential or P²D, it is up to you to cultivate and inspire others to do the same. We must never stop looking to the future and investing in the next generation of leaders that we once saw in ourselves. By reaching back and investing your time, treasures, and talent in the next generation of leaders like the volunteers from Junior Achievement back in St. Louis, you inspire the next generation to become dreamers outside of their current circumstances. When I started IFAS, community outreach was a part of the business plan. I am a firm believer that who we are destined to be is more about leaving an impact on the lives of others.

In chapter 8, "Develop a Growth Mindset," you will learn that there is no easy path to success and that no matter how many times you stumble, getting back up time after time builds the stamina for progress toward your goals. Several well-known leaders who have made mistakes yet have gone on to become individuals that academia and industry use in business case studies as highlighted throughout the book. The takeaway from these stories is that you will learn that what sets CEOs and Presidents of Fortune 100 companies apart from the rest of us as extraordinary leaders is their P^2D and not that they were born with a magical mysterious leadership chromosome. We all have P^2D to some degree or another. It is what we do with it that shapes us as leaders.

Hopefully, after reading this book (that has been in the making for about a decade now), you will see that there are layers to leadership that, once peeled back, will help you discover your true P^2D and what makes you tick as a leader. As you can see in this brief introduction, my growth mindset has been compounded by lessons, both good and bad, throughout my leadership journey. From my Junior Achievement days to the military and then into business, I realized that I cannot lead a team where I was not willing to go physically or mentally. It is also my hope that you walk away with little nuggets that help you enhance, ignite, and live out your P^2D by using past experiences and influences to learn and grow yourself and others around you.

CHAPTER 1

Discover Your P²D

Passion, Perseverance, and Drive P²D

Neither the business school nor this book can instill P²D in you. It is something that must come from within like a light in a lighthouse that shines from every direction no matter where you are standing.

—Tabatha

||||||||||||||||||||||||||||||||||||||||||||||||||||||

Hundreds of thousands of new companies are created by American entrepreneurs every year, and who knows how many millions of employees initiate plans to climb the corporate ladder? Some of these entrepreneurs and employees have small goals, some are aiming so high that it seems outlandish, and others are in-between. Whatever their goals, industries, backgrounds, and talents, they share the feeling that they can change their lives, that they can turn their dreams into reality and become leaders.

Many of those who have already founded profitable companies or have moved up the corporate hierarchy have thoughts as to how they became leaders.

For example, Virginia Rometty, executive chairwoman of IBM, has said that it is important to look for new challenges and set aside the idea of being comfortable in favor of growth.

John D. Rockefeller, the world's very first billionaire, spoke of reaching for the brass ring when urging us to be willing to risk losing the good situation we have to reach for something much better.

Barbara Corcoran, the founder of the Corcoran Group, emphasized the commitment needed to become a leader, saying that when it comes to building a business, if you aren't giving it everything you have to give, you're giving it nothing.

Apple cofounder Steve Jobs highlighted the effort required, especially over the long run, noting that perseverance is the key item separating those who succeed from those who do not.

President Barack Obama highlighted staying power, saying you can't avoid failure; it's inevitable. What matters is whether you respond by giving up or by stepping back into the ring.

Former COO Sheryl Sandberg, addressed resilience, saying that while what you achieve is important, how you survive failure is what will define your life.

These are great, inspirational ideas that, in different ways, highlight the importance of passion, perseverance, and drive. They may use different words to describe these characteristics; but I firmly believe that passion, perseverance, and drive—or what I call P^2D— are the keys to success in life no matter what it is we wish to do. P^2D allows us to lead a business or group, create our company, climb toward and possibly into the C-suite, right social wrongs, break generational curses, and so much more.

Our P^2D determines how we prepare for events and challenges, routine and extraordinary; whether we see setbacks as defeats or lessons; and how firmly we stick to our core beliefs as we are buffeted by life's trials and tribulations. The brighter our P^2D flame burns, the easier it is for us to realize our dreams or achieve our highest potential.

This book is aimed at leaders aspiring to achieve their dreams. They may already be heading companies, divisions, or departments; they may be entrepreneurs with an idea for a new business; or they may be employees eager to scale the ladder and one day head a department, division, or perhaps the entire company. No matter what their position, these leaders and leaders-to-be can benefit from tapping into their P²D with a growth mindset.

We'll talk about ways of keeping our flames burning brightly later on. For now, let's take a look at the three elements of P²D: passion, perseverance, and drive.

Passion: The Thing You Just Can't Get Off Your Mind

Chase down your passion like it's the last bus of the night.

—Terri Guillemets

||||||||||||||||||||||||||||||||||||||||||||||||||||||||||

Passion is the thing we just can't stop thinking about, dreaming about, talking about, and planning for.

We may have a passion for large and strictly personal goals, such as a burning desire to be the best, to make the most money, or to own the biggest business/house/car or what have you.

Your passion may be for a specific activity or field, such as weaving beautiful baskets, playing basketball, opening a business, or being the first to create a sustainable community in outer space. Jeff Bezos, founder of Amazon, and Richard Branson of Virgin Airlines are among the many who have developed a burning passion for taking the human race into the cosmos. They each spent well over a decade researching and developing space vehicles. Bezos paid for the efforts out of his pocket, spending roughly $5.5 billion over twenty years to build the rocket ship that took him for a ten-minute suborbital space ride in 2021. Branson, who beat Bezos into space by less than two weeks, spent some $840 million just on that single fight, not counting all the money he had poured into the years of research and development—plus the inevitable failures along the way.

Where does such passion come from? For Bezos, the dream began during his childhood summer visits to his grandfather, who had worked on space technology for the Atomic Energy Commission in the 1950s and 1960s. As a high schooler, Bezos announced that he wanted to be a space entrepreneur and, as class valedictorian, gave a speech about solving the problems of pollution and overpopulation on Earth by colonizing space. As for Branson, he has said that he has wanted to go into space since he was a child.[1]

For Bezos and Branson, the passion was based on their personal dreams. For others, the passion is more down to earth, concerned with assisting those in need or bringing pleasure to everyday life. This may take the form, for example, of building houses for the homeless or taking in foster children to provide a brighter future for them.

Our P^{2}D burns brightly when we are following our purpose in life: it's a self-energizing cycle, for the act of following our purpose often serves as fuel for our passions, perseverance, and drive. Of course, if what we are the most passionate about takes up most of our time but does not allow us to support ourselves and our families, we have to reconsider how this one thing that we are passionate about fits into our lives. In some cases, our passions can become our professions, but in other cases, if it doesn't provide monetarily for you, it should be considered a hobby. Yes, a *hobby*!

Aligning our purposes with things we are passionate about can help us write our stories the way we want them to go, creating our happy endings.

---

[1] Jonathan Amos, "Sir Richard Branson takes off on 'extraordinary' space flight," BBC.com (July 22, 2021), accessed January 10, 2022, https://www.bbc.com/news/science-environment-57790040.

Perseverance: The Refusal to Stop Driving toward the Passion

*It doesn't matter how many times you get knocked down.
All that matters is you get up one more time than you
were knocked down.*

—Roy T. Bennett

Perseverance is what keeps us going over what may be a very long haul despite the obstacles. Perseverance is the will to continue on even if we have to chip away at a thick brick wall with a tiny tin hammer. Perhaps we've been denied the patent we've sought six times or have been rejected by a dozen companies that we want to do business with. Maybe we've been passed over for promotion numerous times or have repeatedly bombed out on our presentation to the board. These setbacks may be big and painful and may threaten to derail us entirely, but it doesn't matter; we must keep on going.

Perseverance can't be taught in business school, for it comes from within. We build perseverance by looking at times past when we tried and succeeded. We build perseverance by learning about people who pushed on despite tremendous obstacles and then emulating them. And if we think that we lack perseverance, we may notice that we develop a great deal of it when we are motivated or inspired by some external force. We find our perseverance when something turns on that switch within us. Or perhaps someone reminds us of a time we showed perseverance and overcame something. Maybe a friend or spouse sees us struggling and reminds us of who we are and what we've overcome in the past.

Perseverance is strongly tied to our passions and purposes in life. If we find that we just can't persevere in a certain area, it may be because it is not our passion. Or perhaps the timing for this particular goal is off. As Henry Ford once said, failing gives you the chance to start again, this time better prepared because you have learned something from the failure.

Tabatha Turman

Drive: The Conversion of Passion into Action

The man who can drive himself further once the effort gets painful is the man who will win.

—Roger Bannister

|||||||||||||||||||||||||||||||||||||||||||||||||||||||

Drive is the animating force that turns passion into action, that converts the dream into reality.

It may be that our passions are so powerful that our dreams convert themselves into actions automatically. In this case, the drive comes from within. Or perhaps we're driven by external factors, such as the need to provide for our families or to break generational patterns and curses.

A single mother named Bette Nesmith Graham needed money after her divorce, so she took a job as a secretary in a bank. She was later promoted to executive secretary, but that was as far as women were permitted to rise in the banking industry in the 1950s. Back then, in the days of typewriters, it was very difficult to erase errors, so she developed a "paint" used to cover typos. Even though some of her bosses scolded her for using it, other secretaries asked to use it, and she began marketing her Mistake Out in 1956. Operating from her house, she built what became the Liquid Paper Company. The popular typewriter correction fluid company was sold in 1979 for $47.5 million; and when she passed away in 1980, a large chunk of her $50 million estate was used to establish a foundation that supported battered women's shelters, educational scholarships for mature women, and other worthy causes.

Going back even further in time, young Henry Ford was expected to take over the family farm, but he hated farming. He did, however, enjoy taking apart and reassembling pocket watches and loved tinkering with engines and the new horseless carriages that were beginning to appear in the 1890s. It took him a while to get off the farm, but by his late twenties, he had built his first car; and in 1899, he founded his first car company. It failed, but Ford opened another company a few years later. He left that business. Then in 1901, he cofounded what became the Ford Motor Company. One hundred and twenty years later, Ford is still controlled by the Ford family; and as of March 2022, Henry's great-grandson serves as executive chairman.

Both Nesmith and Ford were driven to succeed although for different reasons. Nesmith needed to solve the problems of money and errors while Ford wished to engage his passion. Both were tremendous successes.

Whether sparked by internal or external factors, our drive determines what we are doing, minute after minute, day after day, year after year. Not what we're *thinking* about doing but what we're actually doing. Are we, for example, wasting time on social media? The average American spends over two hours a day scrolling through posts and pictures, happy to see all those likes and smiley faces. That's nice, but unless we need to be on social media for business, we're wasting precious time. Those two hours we lose every day add up to 30.4 days over a year. That's a full month wasted, gone forever. How many contacts could we have made in that month? How much could we have learned? How many times could we have met with our mentors and with others who might support or educate us?

Not only have we lost all that time, but in some cases, we've "gained" something we don't need: a false sense of reality. With carefully curated posts and sites that show people at their best, with filters and hashtags and all the rest, we're looking at a make-believe world. If we aren't grounded, we feel as if we're falling behind our friends, even "friends" we've never met or spoken to and we feel bad about ourselves. Then we feel good when we get a lot of clicks and likes.

Wasting time on social media is like spending the day looking at fun-house mirrors. Everything is distorted, and nothing takes us any closer to our goals. Do you want to be well entertained and popular, or do you want to create a great company? You have to decide. You have to figure out what drives you.

Our drive is strongest when tied to our passion. This makes sense, for when what we *need* to do is what we *want* to do, it's no effort at all. On the other hand, it's difficult to keep pushing ahead and doing something we don't care much about. I have no interest in scuba diving, so I can't get much energy up for doing it. On the other hand, I loved building my company. It was never work to me. I often had to pull myself away from it to attend to other things.

One of the simplest ways to tell if your passion and drive are aligned is to look at what you are actually doing day to day, hour to hour, and minute to minute. For example, you may have a great passion to invent something and earn a patent for it, but what are you doing to turn your dream into reality? Are you actively researching, talking to people in the field, developing prototypes, and doing whatever else is required to invent? Or are you finding excuses not to? If you are not doing what needs to be done, it may be that what you believe to be your passion is simply not your passion. Maybe your passion and actions are misaligned, or the actions you've chosen are not right for you.

You don't have to jump over obstacles all day long to prove that you have the drive, but you do have to do *something*. If you're sitting in your parked car, and your foot is not on the gas pedal, and you're not going anywhere, you don't have any drive. And yes, we can all get sidetracked once in a while. Perhaps a family member becomes ill and requires our care or we lose an important client or a pandemic strikes. Life happens. It takes us in unexpected directions, and our drive may suffer. What matters is how we respond, whether we either get back on track or give it up. Indeed, you can tell how powerful your drive is or how connected it is to your passion when you hit brick walls. Do you give up when you hit the wall? Or do you throw yourself into finding a way through, around, over, or under that wall?

Jack Welch, the former CEO of General Electric, said, "Good business leaders create a vision, articulate the vision, passionately own the vision, and relentlessly drive it to completion."[2] Notice the emphasis Welch placed on drive: it can take relentless drive for us to get where we want to go. Passion itself isn't always enough. Lack of access to good schooling for children from marginalized groups doesn't just go away because we passionately want it to. Attitudes that have made it difficult for women to rise to the top ranks in politics don't resolve on their own, and neither does generational poverty no matter how passionate we are about those issues. Passion tells us where we want to go to solve these issues; however, it's the drive that takes us there.

Behind every solution to a problem, whether large or small, is the drive that turned passion into action.

P²D, in Sum

Passion is the great dream. Drive turns passion into action. Perseverance keeps us moving forward despite the obstacles.

Without passion, it can be difficult to take action. And when obstacles keep blocking us, it can be hard to persevere; our drive may be blunted. The stronger the passion, however, the easier it will be to drive forward despite all obstacles. And the greater the drive and perseverance, the easier it will be to keep the flame of passion burning.

We're all born with passion, perseverance, and drive, to one degree or another, in one mixture of the three or another. In some of us, a strong P²D is obvious from the start or develops early in

---

[2] Noel Tichy and Ram Charan, "Speed, Simplicity, Self-Confidence: An Interview with Jack Welch," *HBR* (March 2, 2020), accessed January 15, 2022, https://hbr.org/1989/09/speed-simplicity-self-confidence-an-interview-with-jack-welch.

life. You might see this, for example, in a young child who eagerly practices over and over to master drawing, soccer, or piano; who decides always to get top marks in school; or who demonstrates great concern for others. In others, the flame of P^2D is not so bright, while for others, it's quite dim. In many of us, the flame that had once burned brightly grows dimmer over time.

Fortunately, we can do quite a bit to strengthen our P^2D. We can even succeed even if our P^2D never blazed brightly, for we can enhance our P^2D in several ways. A powerful way to do so is to learn about and emulate others who succeeded despite facing many obstacles. People such as media giant Oprah Winfrey; Ursula Burns, CEO of Xerox and the first African American woman to head up a Fortune 500 company; freedom fighter Nelson Mandela; mega best-selling author Stephen King, a former slave turned freedom fighter Frederick Douglass; and many more. They all have P^2D, supercharged by a growth mindset.

We'll look at ways to tap into and expand your P^2D and growth mindset in the coming chapters. But first, a word about choices.

CHAPTER 2

Choices and Channeling

It is your choices and decisions that determine your destiny.

—Roy Bennett

|||||||||||||||||||||||||||||||||||||||||||||||||||||

Passion, perseverance, and drive are the keys to success in almost every aspect of life. But don't think it's just a simple matter of finding something you enjoy doing and then plowing ahead full steam, ignoring all problems and conflicts. That can be a recipe for disaster.

One reason for this is that we often have multiple passions, some of which get in each other's way. For example, we may want to create and build a company *and* be a great mom who creates memorable experiences for her children. Both passions are time-intensive, so we may have to prioritize, juggle schedules, work harder, and work smarter at both being a businesswoman and a mom.

In other cases, our passions might conflict with each other. A business owner, faced with employees and potential employees demanding higher wages, may have to decide if it's more important to protect the bottom line or be able to hire the best talent. An inventor who founded a company may have to decide if it's more important to maintain absolute control over his invention or share authority with people who understand the business better than he does. A consultant may want to maintain her price structure yet at the same time wish to sign a new client who can't afford her fee but would allow her to move into a new industry. She has to decide which is more important: profits or expanding access to clients.

I know that I have to balance my conflicting desires to break the generational curses and create and grow a business against my strong desire to give back to the community. My solution is to defer giving as much as I would like to give now, so I can give even more later. I am also very passionate about creating other business ventures and have to discipline myself to stay put and finish what I'm doing before creating something new. Otherwise, I'll wind up splitting my focus and failing at both endeavors.

I love fashion and some years ago decided to open an online boutique. "Everyone is doing it," I told myself. "How difficult can it be?" Little did I know that marketing and sourcing the right items would consume so much time! At one point, I thought outsourcing would do the trick; however, as the owner of a startup, there is only so much I could outsource. The boutique did well, but I made the conscious decision to put it on the back burner for now because the time required to grow the company to the level I wanted to was competing with my time to continue growing IFAS. It was a tough pill to swallow but very necessary. I learned that to have a passion for fashion is one thing, and to build a thriving e-commerce business is a totally different thing.

It's often necessary to choose between passions because we don't live one life experience at a time. Instead, life is often a confusing jumble. We may have to deal with work, schooling, aging parents, and a family of our own. And we certainly have to deal with changes in technology and economic conditions, plus pandemics and other factors we have no control over.

We shouldn't feel like failures when we can't give 100 percent to everything or when we have to postpone one thing to succeed with another. Instead, we can try to devise new ways of dealing with conflicting goals. I spent years building my business. There were many times when I wanted to attend my children's game or track meets but also had to be out on the road servicing my clients or seeking new opportunities. I found that sometimes it just wasn't possible to arrange my life so I could be a great mother *and* a great businesswoman—at least not in the traditional way.

So I made choices and developed new ways. I would get photos and video clips of my children sent to me by other parents in attendance. Later, I would watch the video with them, applaud them, and relive the game as they watched themselves in action. And when I did go to the games, I was their number one fan and still am, although they are adults. I would leave my cell phone in the car and run up and down the sidelines as they raced up and down the football or track field or basketball court. When I was there, I was present—really present—and they knew and appreciated it. Once, my oldest stopped in the middle of a basketball game, looked up into the stands where I was talking to another parent, and yelled, "Clap, Mommy, clap!" Everyone in the stands and on the court heard that, and they all stopped and watched as I clapped for what seemed like an eternity. That was a lesson for me about how much my presence actually meant in my children's life. A friend has told me that when he was young, his father, a doctor trying to build his practice, was super busy, leaving the house early in the morning and often working late into the night. But every Sunday at noon, when my friend and his siblings walked out of Sunday school, their father was standing by the car, waiting to take them to lunch and the park. My friend said that even at age seven, he knew how difficult it was for his father to get away from the hospitals and sick patients, and he loved his dad for doing it. You can create new traditions as long as you're showing your effort and how much you care.

Remember, making choices doesn't mean that we are failures. I don't subscribe to the theory that we can have perfect balance in life, that we can accomplish all our goals all the time. The truth is, there are often six different things on our to-do list that have to be done—right now! This means we're going to have to pick when to give time and energy to one item and when to the next. We can't feel guilty about this, for guilt saps our energy. And we can't let other negative emotions get in our way. For example, we can't resent elderly parents when we stop living our passion to take care of them. Instead, we must realize that sometimes there is a purposeful shift in our lives that causes us to detour, albeit for a worthy cause. Caring for our parents was what we had to do at the moment, what we chose to do. We can feel good about making them our priority for now and then moving back to other items on our list later.

Channeling Your P²D

P²D is the key to success in every aspect of life. But it is not alone. Our passion, perseverance, and drive must be harnessed and directed to produce practical results. In other words, P²D must be carefully channeled. We do this by drawing upon our experiences, tools, and relationships as resources for "translating" our P²D into practical, tangible success.

Many people automatically channel their P²D. Many of the rest of us, unfortunately, fail to do so because we don't understand the value of the things or situations that derailed us in the past. We don't use them as lessons and tools to help us get started, to persevere when getting back on track to realizing a dream that was deferred. In a sense, we're "blocked off" from these tools. This can happen for many reasons:

1. **Overreliance on formal education**—perhaps we've been college educated, and the experiences we're facing in real life don't look like what we were taught in school. After all, textbooks don't dwell on the stress of suddenly being assigned to head a project you know nothing about, having to study up on it fast, struggling to improve your public speaking skills because you must soon present it to the board, getting turned down by the board multiple times, and putting in endless hours before finally succeeding. The

truth is, by doing all this, we've developed a tremendous amount of real-world experience. In particular, we have learned how to be told no multiple times yet to keep pushing ahead until we succeed. They don't teach you that in school. Unfortunately, many people let their textbook learning define their horizons and hold them back.

2. **Improper assessment of our toolkit called life**—many of us simply don't believe that what success we have had was due to our efforts. Instead, we think our success was due to someone else, circumstances, or luck. We just can't believe that it was our leadership, insight, determination, and other factors that guided the team forward to make it happen, that allowed us to come up with the clever way of solving the problem or gave us the strength to keep moving forward when doing so was difficult.

3. **Embarrassment and shame**—most of us don't want to face the shameful, wasteful, or hurtful things we have done in the past and don't want others to find out about them. So we suppress our past, not realizing that our past experiences have been driving us to be successful. Rather than suppressing, we could be converting our embarrassment and fear into passion, perseverance, and drive to be someone else, someone much better than we were. We could use our past to prove to ourselves—and to others—that we're not that person anymore.

Larry Miller is a friend and confidant of basketball great Michael Jordan, as well as president of the Portland Trail Blazers and chairman of the Jordan Brand. He is an incredibly successful man with a challenging past: In 1965, at the age of sixteen, he deliberately shot and killed a young man—a boy really, just eighteen years old. Miller served his time in jail, was released, and turned his life around. He became educated, befriended Michael Jordan, and rose quite high in the worlds of sports and business. Presumably, he was trying to get as far away from the boy he was, and that helped make him into a tremendously successful man. He kept that terrible secret for fifty-six years until he shared it with the world in a 2021 interview with *Sports Illustrated*. And he candidly admitted his guilt, saying there was absolutely no reason for him to have taken the other man's life. He's been haunted by what he did for decades and feared revealing his secret would destroy the friendships and fortune he spent years building. But his big mistake, terrible as it was, did not define his destiny.

Unfortunately, many of us go in the opposite direction, blocking and hiding from our shame. It's as if we have a parrot on our shoulder, constantly whispering that we can never be successful because of the one terrible thing we did. And we respond by telling ourselves, "They're not going to accept me. They're not going to like me because of what I did." We refuse to acknowledge the dumb/embarrassing/hurtful thing we did, and we fail to use the energy and passion it can generate to make ourselves into better people.

Filmmaker Paul Schrader once noted that if you want to be creative, you have to learn how to "feel at ease with your embarrassment." I believe that feeling at ease with your embarrassments and shame is equally important in your business life, family life, and all other aspects of life.

4. **Desire to "leave the past behind"**—this is not about the things we've done. Instead, it's about what others have done to us. Life treated us poorly as children, failed us as teachers, and disappointed us in relationships. We don't want to have anything to do with these past experiences, don't even want to think about them. But the terrible things that have happened to us often contain rich lessons about our resilience, perseverance, and more.

5. **Lack of knowledge on how to triangulate**—we don't take a challenging experience from the past such as raising kids and apply the same will and determination to another endeavor. We think our experiences were irrelevant to the challenges we are facing today.

6. **Lack of mentorship/guidance**—no one is making it clear to us that drawing on certain experiences could be helpful. It's not always obvious how to channel and apply our past experiences. In fact, it's not always obvious that we even have relevant experiences to apply. It may take a mentor to point out that the leadership skills you developed in the military, for example, can be applied in many different businesses. Your military leadership skills may be so valuable that a company will be willing to train you in the specifics of the business because they are desperate for leaders such as you. A good mentor often sees much more potential and promise in you than you do and can point it out.

The key thing to understand is that even a strong P^2D can meander down the wrong path or may dim over time. That's why it is so important to be aware of your passion, perseverance, and drive and work with them deliberately. It's a two-way street: you help your P^2D, and it will help you.

Plans Are Not Perfect

Champions keep playing until they get it right.
—Billie Jean King

We may be born with a powerful dose of P^2D, but even a very brightly lit P^2D can be dimmed by life events. It may be battered by COVID-like pandemics, an economic depression, divorce, job termination, bankruptcy, kids, horrible experiences with bad bosses or partners, natural disasters, and a life without purpose. Or maybe we get into career paths that seem good at first but are not compatible with our purpose. I once saw a cartoon of an elephant standing next to a tree and being told to start climbing. While I found this quite amusing, there's no way an elephant can climb a tree, for the task and tools are simply not aligned. Trapped in misalignments like this, we feel that we simply can't succeed, that we're no good and will never succeed.

Many of us try to stay on track by developing a business plan for our work life and game plans for education, relationships, and other aspects of life. But no plan can cover everything, for we can't anticipate everything. Who would have thought that in 2020, the shelves in U.S. grocery stores would be stripped bare by a virus that began on the other side of the world?

Unfortunately, we often become wed to the thing right in front of our eyes, which is the great plan we think will be our salvation. In the corporate arena, think of Blockbuster, which went from being the biggest video rental company in the nation to filing for bankruptcy. Blockbuster could easily have outmaneuvered Netflix, but it was stuck on its business plan. It didn't see the new trends in technology and society creeping up on the sides. Blockbuster could have bought Netflix, Redbox, and other competitors and remained on top. But the company executives were so fixated on their preset plan that they missed many opportunities to adapt to changing conditions.

Blockbuster is a textbook example of what happens when you insist on sticking firmly to the plan even when conditions are changing. The first Blockbuster, which opened in the mid-1980s, offered customers thousands and thousands of videos to rent compared to the few hundred found in neighborhood rental stores back then. By 1992, Blockbuster was the category giant, with 2,800 stores in the United States and the UK. In 1999, Blockbuster, now boasting 6,000 stores worldwide, went public. But there was already reason to question the plan. Two years previously, in 1997, a rival video rental company called Netflix was created. Its founder, like most everyone else who rented from Blockbuster, was tired of paying Blockbuster's exorbitant late fees.

Netflix offered a large library of films to rent without late fees. In addition, Netflix mailed the videos to your house, so you didn't have to go to a store to get them. Blockbuster had the opportunity to purchase Netflix but decided not to. Then, in 2000, yet another competitor with a different approach appeared in the form of Redbox. The film selection in those ubiquitous red boxes was small, but the Redboxes, stationed by grocery and convenience stores, were easy to find and quick to use.

Still, Blockbuster wasn't worried. Why should it be? In 2004, company revenues from its 9,000 stores totaled $5.9 billion. That same year, it launched an online video rental store. But it was already too late, for they were way behind Netflix. Even eliminating the hated late fees didn't help as Blockbuster lost 75 percent of its market value by 2005, filed for bankruptcy in 2010, and closed all of it remaining stores in 2013.

Blockbuster failed to see how nimble competitors could use the Internet and red rental boxes to undermine their market share and failed to understand how much their customers hated those horrible late fees. It couldn't make the necessary hard choices.

We must always remember that any plan is a living document. It must evolve as life moves ahead and conditions change. Otherwise, we'll be hit by something unexpected—or something we should have expected but didn't—and wind up like Blockbuster, Borders Books, Toys "R" Us, Lord & Taylor, Radio Shack, Pan Am Airways, and other industry giants that failed miserably.

The P²D Forecaster

There's an army expression they teach during marksmanship training that tells you to look constantly to the right and to the left to scan your sector. That's a reminder that you have to be aware of everything in your blind spots, not just what's happening right in front of your eyes. Making business plans and game plans is a great idea, but we can't insist on following them exactly to the letter. After all, the plan is a working document that may need to be adapted as circumstances change. We can't ignore shifts in our industry, career paths, life goals, etc. We can't ignore what's happening on the right and left of our chosen sectors. If conditions have changed, we must be nimble enough to change with them.

That's where the P²D forecaster can be helpful. The P²D forecaster helps us understand our strengths and weaknesses in terms of internal beliefs and external forces. For the forecaster, we use a diagram like the one that follows. On the left side, we look at our internal P²D forces—our belief system—in terms of fortitude and vulnerabilities. On the right side, we examine the external forces that can affect our P²D, which are the prospects and risks. Working through the Forecaster helps us remain mindful of how what we believe hinders us from moving ahead with our plans and what factors are creating obstacles, interfering with our decisions as we move out on our P²D.

Like the SWOT (strengths, weaknesses, opportunities, and threats) analysis performed by businesses, the P²D forecaster is a powerful tool for our personal lives. Not only does it force us to think through the internal and external forces influencing our thoughts and behaviors, but it also allows us to keep reanalyzing the situation as conditions change.

Performing a P²D forecast is simple. Take a piece of paper and divide it into sections. You don't have to do anything fancy. Just jot out the headings "P²D Internal Forces" and "P²D Perceived External Forces" and indicate sections for fortitude, vulnerabilities, prospects, and risks.

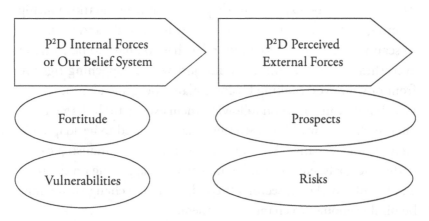

Then list the appropriate items in each category. Here's what I came up with in a P²D forecaster after I had started IFAS:

My Fortitude:

- determination to break generational curses
- strong worth ethic
- ability to connect with all kinds of people
- education, both formal and informal
- real-world federal financial management experience
- ability to maintain relationships with military leaders that I once worked with when they transitioned to the private sector

My Vulnerabilities:

- feeling inadequate, for I had never built a business before and this was a whole new arena for me
- young family to take care of and support
- tendency to become unfocused when trying to handle too many things at once, not focusing on strategic areas, not knowing where my time was most valuable
- tendency to burn out
- the difficulty of translating and transferring military defense financial management experience to civilian federal agencies needs

My Prospects:

- I had a reliable network from the military.
- Being a veteran provided me with opportunities to work with the government.
- We were at the height of the war in Iraq, which meant there was a need for what my company had to offer.

My Risks:

- competitors
- low barrier to entry into an oversaturated market
- lack of enough access to capital
- changing market conditions
- customer spending habits were more focused on wartime effort when I began and less focused as time went on

There is no set number of items to put in each of the four areas. There are no right or wrong answers, and there are no instant solutions. It's a thought exercise. Be absolutely truthful, for if you fudge your answers, the only person you're trying to fool is yourself.

Think through your P²D forecast thoroughly, asking yourself what you can do to take advantage of your fortitude and probabilities while shoring up your vulnerabilities and watching for any risks that have been foreshadowed. Look at your forecaster at least once a year, for you must periodically remind yourself of what you have learned from it. And reevaluate it at least once every six months, for conditions change rapidly, and you may have to change as well. Your forecast is like a window into your soul, so be careful who you share it with. Only show it to people who can give you solid feedback and constructive criticism, such as mentors (see the following bullet point "Limiting Who We Share With").

As I learned during marksmanship training in the army, you must always scan your sectors. Always look to your right and left. The same applies in business. You have a goal, which is your target, be it a client you want to acquire, a new market you wish to enter or dominate, and so on. You know you have to look straight ahead to find the things in your way that might stop you. But you always have to look to the right and the left, to the "white spaces in the page margins," to find the not-so-obvious risks.

The lesson for us is that we must always be ready to make choices, to find different and sometimes new ways to channel our P²D. Our choices, our willingness to look to the right and left while scanning our sectors, and our ability to adapt to changing circumstances—positive and negative—these are the things that help keep our P²D burning bright.

And Then There Are the Practical Things to Do

Good luck is when opportunity meets preparation.
—Eliyahu Goldratt

|||||||||||||||||||||||||||||||||||||||||||||||

It's important to understand what P²D is and how it works. But that's not enough. We must also get practical and do things that enhance, develop, nourish, and protect our passion, perseverance, and drive. There are many ways to do this:

- **Invest in ourselves**—we are our own key assets. We have our brains and brawn, our ability to learn and lead, and our willingness to respond to changes and to bounce back when things have gone poorly. We must continually improve our key assets by investing in ourselves.

  Investing in ourselves means getting the formal education necessary to move ahead, as well as the informal education and experience that cannot be taught in school. It means staying physically fit so we can withstand long hours, grueling road trips, and more. It means looking after our mental well-being, for life can be very challenging. Investing in ourselves means developing a positive mindset to get us through the inevitable setbacks.

- **Limit who we share with**—we are heavily influenced by what the five people closest to us think about us and what we're doing. But these five folks probably don't have our vision and dream; they can't see it. They're likely to quiz us, to challenge and critique our vision and actions. We have to be careful with who we share our passion and to who we talk about what we're doing to turn our passion into reality. It doesn't take much—a negative comment, a laughing dismissal—to dim our flame. Words matter! That's why we must only share with those who share our vision or at least support it. At the same time, we want to surround ourselves with people we trust and respect who can provide honest feedback that we will receive and accept as constructive criticism when warranted.

- **Find mentors**—we draw enormous comfort and strength from talking to and being with people who have traveled the path we wish to journey, who have been successful in this area, and who have had a dream like ours. We need to get in to meet them and, when we do, to listen carefully to them. Find out what their struggles and pitfalls were. Be a sponge and soak up everything they have to say, for this is our time to learn, be inspired, and grow. And we must be sure to have an "ask," a request for something. Our ask may be a suggestion for a pertinent book to read, an opportunity to shadow the person for a day, an introduction to someone in the field, or anything else that advances us. We should never be shy about asking! If you ask, you may be refused. But if you don't ask, you're refusing yourself the chance to move ahead.

- **Be intentional with our time**—being intentional with our time means using it to our best advantage. It means doing what we say we'll do, breaking goals down into smaller steps so they don't seem overwhelming, checking them off as they are accomplished; being accountable to ourselves, and getting an accountability partner if we struggle with this. We can't accomplish what we need to accomplish when we are lazy or when we give up just half a step shy of realizing the dream.

- **Actively claim, rather than passively accept, our destiny**—imagine two siblings with an alcoholic father. One child grows to be an alcoholic, like the father, while the second becomes a successful business person. They both came from the exact same family situation and the same educational and socioeconomic level. They had similar genes yet wildly different outcomes. This can happen when people internalize their unhappy childhood. They think that it was all doom and gloom and that they are destined to be like their father. But other people tell themselves that while their fathers went down one path, they are deliberately heading down a different one. They choose to be great. They choose to acknowledge their life experiences but do not claim them as their destiny. Two different children from identical situations. Two different mindsets. Each mindset turned into a self-fulfilling prophecy.

- **Build a network**—we need people. We need mentors, advocates, parents, employees, siblings, and others to help us, motivate us, provide resources, and connect us with others who can help us advance. No one goes all the way as a one-person team. No matter how much we think it's all about us, at the end of the day, we need people to push us further.

  That's why networks are so important. We must always look for people who are aligned with our goals and where we want to go. We must hang in these clusters; join the appropriate organizations; and be present, be seen, serve on committees, and otherwise add value—that's how to network with intention (see chapter 4 for more on networking).

- **Be intentional with relationships**—it doesn't help us just to use people, to add them to our network, and only to call on them when we need them. It doesn't help them either. Relationships work best when they are two-way, which is why you must always be asking yourself, "How can I add value to this person's life? What can I do to help them?" You might think you have nothing to offer a successful mentor, but you can send them a note on their birthday. You can send them favorite bag of popcorn from their hometown or something similar. You can find a way to show gratitude for the people in your life, and it often takes only a small gesture to produce big results in terms of adding value to someone's life.

- **Rise above**—many of us come from challenging circumstances. But we can never allow ourselves to be bound by our familial socioeconomic status and habits. We can never believe that because our ancestors lived a certain way, we have to do so as well.

Rising above can be difficult for some, but there are countless inspiring examples of people helping others do just that. Things were not looking good for Timothy Harrison who walked to work at Waffle House, arriving at 7:00 a.m. on the day he was to graduate from Woodland High School in Alabama.[3] His manager was surprised to see him, knowing that this was graduation day. But Timothy didn't have a ride to the ceremony or tickets to get in. And since he had had to work during the graduation rehearsal, he didn't get the cap and gown he needed to wear to graduation. But his manager told the young man to contact the school and say he'd be there. One of Timothy's fellow employees drove him to the school to get the cap and gown while the others pooled their money to buy Harrison a new suit. The Waffle House's assistant manager went and bought Timothy nice clothes despite the fact that it was her day off. And when Timothy came back from the graduation ceremony,

---

[3] Christine Fernando, "Teen thought he'd miss his high school graduation. His Waffle House 'family' wouldn't let him," *USA Today* (June 20, 2021), accessed November 22, 2021, https://www.usatoday.com/story/news/nation/2021/06/20/waffle-house-co-workers-get-alabama-student-high-school-graduation/7757649002/.

all the employees went out to the parking lot to greet and congratulate him.

Rising above can be difficult, but there are many people willing to help. Of course, we must be willing to be helped. We must believe we deserve an assist. We have to be willing to learn and take from other people, to be forever learners eager to learn from many different sources, and to recognize when it's time to ask for assistance.

We may have wonderful ideas but be overly prideful and unwilling to have outsiders come in and share in the profits or the credit. We may think we know it all and can do it all or that others can't possibly see things the way we do. But the reality is that we need other people. With the right people on the team, we can go further faster. So we have to be willing to ask for help and to value what every team member brings. And we never have to worry that asking for help will diminish us in any way. If we are, for example, a founding business owner, we need not worry about our title as founder being taken away. We can give others all the accolades they deserve yet remain the original creator, the one who came up with the idea and put in all the sweat and tears necessary to get things going. It's okay not to be the smartest person in the room; in fact, it's a good thing to surround yourself with very smart people who know and can do things we cannot as a leader. If you're the smartest person in the room who knows it all as a leader, you haven't built your team the right way. But if you have built it properly—that is, filled your team with talented people who complement your shortcomings—then nine times out of ten, you will not be the smartest person in the room. And that's a very good thing.

These tips, in brief, are how we apply the theory of P^2D. Now, let's take a closer look at the key steps we can take to reach and then surpass our potential.

Key Points

- P^2D is like raw power: it must be carefully channeled to carry us toward our goals. We channel our P^2D by drawing on our experiences, tools, and relationships.
- We will be forced to make choices at various times. Having to choose between two paths is never a failure. Instead, it's an opportunity to move ahead in a stronger way.
- It's important to lay out business plans and equally important to amend and evolve them as circumstances change.
- Working through the P^2D forecaster helps us think through the internal forces influencing our behavior, as well as the external forces we must deal with, and respond appropriately.
- In the end, our lives are built on the choices we make on whether we choose wisely and whether we choose to unleash and enhance our passion, perseverance, and drive.

CHAPTER 3

Build Your Brand

Products are made in a factory but brands are created in the mind.

—Walter Landor

"Build a better mousetrap, and the world will beat a path to your door."

That bit of wisdom is ascribed to American philosopher Ralph Waldo Emerson, and unfortunately, it's not true. It may have been true when Emerson proclaimed it in the late 1800s. But back then, there weren't nearly as many entrepreneurs and established businesses in this country, and people dealt mostly in local or regional markets, so it was a lot easier to become known. Today, there are so many existing businesses, and so many starting up every day, that it's difficult for a newcomer to become known, let alone stand out. Making it even more difficult, not only do we have to carve out a niche—or create an entirely new one—among American businesses, but we also have to compete with entrepreneurs and enterprises from all around the world.

And we're not just competing for clients or customers. We're also competing for financing, suppliers, partners, employees, and more. So how do we stand out and become so trusted and admired that people will beat a path to our door?

The best way to do this is to build a great personal brand. A brand does two things: it tells the world who you are and why you're worth engaging with, and it constantly reminds you of who and what you are striving to be.

The story of Dan Price, the cofounder and CEO of Gravity Payments, is a great example of personal branding. In 2015, Price was confronted by one of the employees at his credit card processing company who said he was barely making enough money to get by while Price was receiving $1.1 million a year. Price thought about it for a few days. He realized that he had long been patting himself on the back for treating his employees well, yet some of them were barely scraping along. Price also remembered that the idea of fairness had prompted him to create Gravity Payments in the first place, for he was horrified at the high fees small bar owners had to pay to large financial firms every time someone swiped a credit card at their establishments.

So Price announced that he would, over a few years, raise the minimum wage at Gravity Payments and the other company he owned to $70,000 per year, and lower his salary to the same $70,000. To do so, he drained his retirement accounts and mortgaged both his home and another property he owned. That's a powerful statement, right from the heart! And it established a powerful brand: Dan Price is the boss who believes in treating employees well.

The story of the CEO who slashed his pay went viral. People were eager to work for Price, who received over four thousand résumés in the first week. One of them came from an executive at Yahoo who was so inspired by his action that she quit her job and went to work for Price even though she took a gigantic pay cut. Soon, new customer inquiries rose from thirty to two thousand per month, revenue growth doubled, worker retention rose, and the customer retention rate rose by four percentage points. When the COVID pandemic hit in 2020, almost all of Price's employees volunteered to take a wage cut to keep the company alive, and several dozen said they were willing to see their salaries cut in half! Thanks in large part to this tremendous employee support, Gravity Payments survived the worst of the pandemic and is rebuilding.

Dan Price didn't invent a better mousetrap. Instead, he built an incredible personal brand, and the world came knocking on his door.

What Is a Brand?

Don't be scared to present the real you to the world.
Authenticity is at the heart of success.

—Unknown

|||||||||||||||||||||||||||||||||||||||||||||||||

Think of your brand as being your story, as in "London is a dedicated, determined entrepreneur who always finds a way around obstacles and will succeed." Here's another example: "Wade is friendly and has a way of making people feel at ease."

At its best, your personal brand represents who you truly are, what you value, and what value you bring to others and to organizations. It's not marketing fluff, some slogan you slap on your literature and then forget all about. Your brand is the outer manifestation of the inner you. It's made up of your thoughts, words, and actions. It embraces your values and attitudes and includes the manner in which you bring these to life in your everyday actions. It's your calling card, your billboard proclaiming to the world who you are. Your brand doesn't "tell" people why they should work with you, buy from you, loan money to you, or be associated with you in some other way. That's advertising. Instead, your brand *inspires* people to do so because they trust and admire you.

Your brand attracts people who share your values, admire you, want to purchase from you, work for or with you, mentor you, bring you on their team, or recommend you to others. But a brand isn't just a meaningless mantra or slogan you repeat to everyone you meet. Your brand must represent the genuine you, or people will see through it. If you tell people that your brand is a "team player," but you show up for meetings late and spread gossip about your team members, people will quickly realize that your brand is phony. But if you show up for meetings on time and well prepared, participate in the discussions, support other team members, and then do what you have promised to do for the team, your brand will ring true.

At its essence, branding yourself means telling the truth about yourself. You can fake it till you make it to a certain extent, but if there's no reality behind the image, people will see through it soon enough.

Finding Your Brand

Build your brand for the career you want, not the job you have.

—Dan Schawbel

The very first step in branding yourself is to ask yourself what you want to be known as. Imagine that you're writing your eulogy: How would you like to be remembered when you're gone as being smart, caring, bold, or visionary?

Thinking through how you want to be remembered tells you what's really important to you today. If, for example, you want to be remembered for being super rich, then you will be driven to amass money. Therefore, trying to create a brand as a boss who first and foremost cares about his workers' welfare wouldn't work for you. People will see through it. And even if they don't, trying to be the kind of boss you're not will be too stressful, and you'll give it up soon enough. If, on the other hand, you think about your eulogy and decide that you want to be remembered for your generosity and teamwork, then adopting a generous team-player brand today will be easy and comfortable. After all, it's who you really want to be.

Spend some time thinking about how you would like to be remembered. Take the time to write your eulogy just as you would like it to be presented at your funeral. Think about this person you're describing. Are you that person? If not, can you become that person? Would being that person be a comfortable fit? And if you are that person, or you become that person, can you turn your dreams into reality?

Suppose, for example, that you really want to be remembered for your "damn the torpedoes, full speed ahead" approach. That's really you. But you're trying to climb the ladder in a very stodgy corporation that prides itself on taking the slow, careful approach to everything. Your "damn the torpedoes" brand is true to you, but is it a good fit with your goal in this company? Will it work?

Or suppose you want to be eulogized for being great to your employees and also dream of founding a company that happens to be in a very cyclical industry. You know that you'll have to keep a tight rein on salaries and benefits and will lay lots of people off many times as your company goes through inevitable cycles of expansion and contraction. Is your "boss who is great to employees" brand a good fit for your dream?

If your brand works well with the person you want to be and with your goals, great! If not, you have to rethink your brand, your goals, or both.

What Brand Do You Have?

If you're not branding yourself, you can be sure others do it for you.

—Unknown

||||||||||||||||||||||||||||||||||||||||||||||||||||||

Everyone has a brand, whether they know it or not. Before you've opened your new business or asked for a promotion at work, you have a brand. Even if you've done nothing to create one and have never even thought about it, you already have a brand. And as soon as you step into a room, get on the video conference, join a work team, or otherwise engage with people, they start clueing in to your brand.

Your brand is what people think of you and what they say about you when you're not in the room. If you're an assistant who always attends to tasks immediately and finishes them properly and exactly according to specifications, then your brand is "fast and competent, diligent, and reliable." You may not know it, but that's what the people you work for and with think about you, and it's what they say about you when you're not present. There're happy to have you on their team, and your boss will be happy to take you with them as they move up the ranks.

If, on the other hand, you're an entrepreneur who argues with employees, partners, and most everyone else, your brand is "confrontational and hard to work with." People will work for you if they need the money and will work with you if they think they can profit from the association. But no one will go out on a limb for you. They won't do any more than it takes to keep the checks coming.

You may think you have no control over what people think and say about you. The truth is, you have a tremendous say over that because people are usually pretty accurate in their assessments of you, especially when these assessments consistently come from people who don't know each other. Yes, you might be misunderstood on occasion, and it's possible that someone is deliberately sabotaging your reputation. But for the most part, people know who you are. They look at what you do, listen to what you say, and create your brand.

How do you know what your existing brand is? Pay attention to the common themes in your life. What do people repeatedly say to you or about you? What have your yearly appraisals looked like? If you're in business, what have clients/customers said about you as a leader? What reputation have you built in the community?

Another way to uncover your existing brand is to think about how people respond to you. For example:

- When you step into a leadership position, do people follow you? If so, is it because they want to or have to?
- Do people ask you for guidance or advice? Or do they seem to resent it when you offer advice, argue, or ignore you?
- When people give you assignments, do they emphasize over and over that it needs to be completed in a certain way or by a certain time? Or do they mention the parameters just once and seem glad that you're the one handling it?
- Are people often hesitant when you ask for a letter of recommendation?
- Do you often get referrals based on positive responses from former clients?

There are many more questions you could ask yourself. The key point is to think about how people respond to you: that's your existing brand.

Is this brand what you thought it would be? Or is there a big difference between your perception and reality? If so, why? There are two likely possibilities. One, there's a mismatch between your perception of your brand and the reality of your brand. For example, you might tell yourself that you're a go-getter and then spend hours a day focusing on tasks that are not aligned with your goals or purpose in life. Or you may tell yourself that you'll fearlessly do whatever it takes to make connections but shy away from networking events. You may tell yourself that you are eager to get the best advice possible but dismiss the guidance people give you when you ask. If you're caught in self-conflicts such as these, you're not the brand you think you are.

Uncovering a mismatch is not a disaster. In fact, it's a good thing because for your brand to work, it has to be true to the real you and align with your P^2D. Discovering the mismatch gives you two options: rethink your brand or do what it takes to become the brand you desire.

Another possible reason that your brand is not what you thought it was is that you're doing something to obscure the real you. Are you, for example, putting on a show of bravado to cover up some shortcomings you think you have? Or taking on tasks you know you'll struggle with because you want others to think you're the master of it all? Are you masking your intelligence and drive because you think you have to be "nice"? Are you not speaking up at meetings because you are passionate about a certain topic and don't like to come across as being too aggressive? Doing things such as these will create confusion about your brand.

Always remember that the best brand is the one that's true to you. You can change yourself to a certain extent. You can learn to become a better speaker and acquire other skills, but at the end of the day, there's a certain "essential you" that must be respected, for it cannot be changed. If you're faced with a choice between the "essential you" and the heroic, all-conquering brand you've dreamed of becoming, go with the essential you. There's tremendous strength in truth.

Broadcasting Your Brand

It's a poor dog that doesn't wag its own tail.
—Unknown

|||||||||||||||||||||||||||||||||||||||||||||||||||||||||

Let's assume for now that you know what brand you'd like to have and have discovered what brand you already have, and the two are the same. That is, the brand you want to have is identical to the brand you already have. That's a great start. Now you'd like to broadcast your brand—that is, make many people aware of your brand. How do you go about it?

The quick answer is that you broadcast your brand by living it. Make sure that everything you do and say is consistent with your brand, whether at work, at home, or on social media.

Broadcasting your brand means acting according to your brand. If you're an employee with a "go-getter" brand, you must arrive at work on time and with a smile on your face, always be prepared, finish your tasks on time if not earlier, be willing to stay late if necessary, offer to help others, take advantage of opportunities to learn more, and otherwise show your go-getter spirit and energy. Ask for informational interviewers with higher-ups and with laterals in other departments. Request cross-training to make you more valuable to the company and stay up with industry trends.

Broadcasting your brand means always showing up dressed for the role you want to be. You may prefer jeans over a suit, but if a suit fits your brand, that's what you wear. It goes the other way too. If you prefer to be dressed stylishly but casual clothing best fits your brand, then dress casually. You're dressing for success by presenting yourself as the visual embodiment of your brand. If you want to be a leader, dress like a leader. Dress how you want to be addressed.

Broadcasting your brand means always being prepared. You don't just show up at a meeting; you plan for it. You find out who will be there and what will be discussed, and you study up on the people and topic. If you're going to present, you write it out and practice it over and over, so you'll be pitch perfect. Even if your brand is "casual and off-the-cuff," you still want to be well prepared for the presentation. As the famous author and speaker Mark Twain said, "It usually takes me more than three weeks to prepare a good impromptu speech."

Broadcasting your brand means being cognizant of the things you do and say and what you post on social media. You can't have one brand on social media and another in real life. Be aware of what you like and comment on because that lasts forever. And be intentional. Don't rant and rave—in person or online—about arbitrary things because you had a bad day, for ultimately, that will reflect on your brand.

Broadcasting your brand means considering the company you keep, even family members. You are judged, fairly or not, by the company you keep; and if their attitudes, appearances, views, and more don't mesh with your brand, they will detract from your brand. That doesn't mean you have to disengage from family members who conflict with your brand. You can go to family occasions even with those you disagree with or whose ideology clashes with yours. But if someone is throwing a rally for something you strongly don't believe in, I don't care if it's your mother or grandmother, if it's in conflict with your brand, that's a nonstarter. Don't even think of going. Disengage.

Broadcasting your brand means sprinkling humble mentions of it in your conversation. But always remember the "humble" part of humble mentions; else, you come off as a braggart or narcissist.

Broadcasting your brand means consistently showing up in a manner congruent with your brand.

In brief, broadcasting your well-developed brand means living it with every word and action. Your brand becomes your lifestyle; your lifestyle becomes your brand. This means being your brand at every moment and with every breath: at work, at home, online, at church, on the playing field, in the market, with your friends. You can't be on-brand at the meeting and off-brand at the park, on-brand during the Zoom call and off-brand while tweeting. Neither can you be on-brand with potential financial backers and off-brand with employees. Your brand must be so much *you* that you live it with ease and broadcast it with absolute sincerity. If it's a mask you put on now and then, people will see right through it. Or one day, you'll forget to put it on and be exposed as a phony.

When you broadcast your brand, people will start to see you as a leader, team player, tech wiz, or whatever your brand may be. And your brand will be sincere because you are walking in your true purpose in line with your P^2D.

Building Your Brand

It takes 20 years to build a reputation and five minutes to ruin it.
If you think about that, you'll do things differently.
                                                              —Warren Buffett

|||||||||||||||||||||||||||||||||||||||||||||||||||||||||||||

Broadcasting your brand to the people you come in contact with in your everyday activities is a great start. The next step is to broadcast your brand to a wider audience, in person and via the media and the Internet. There are several steps you can take to do this:

- **Think about who you want to attract**—at any given time, you may be looking for different connections. Perhaps you'd like to find a mentor now, and next year, you'll be looking for angel investors. This means that you have to market different aspects of your brand at different times. It's not a matter of changing your brand. Rather, it's highlighting certain parts or pieces of your brand to specific audiences. Think of your brand as being a buffet table with each plate representing an aspect of your brand. At different times, you'll serve up different dishes, depending on whom you've invited to dinner. All the food in the buffet is true to you. It's just a matter of deciding what to highlight for different people and at different times.
- **Hone your elevator pitch(es)**—you often have but a few moments to introduce yourself to people, so you want to be able to showcase your qualities and value in just a few sentences. Write, edit, and rewrite your pitch until it sparkles. Practice saying it until you are certain you can deliver it in all kinds of situations, such as at a networking event where people are paying attention because it's your

turn to speak, at a party where people are distracted, and at the end of a seminar when people are anxious to get home. Work up variations of your pitch, so you have slightly different versions for when you meet potential mentors, customers, partners, and so on.

- **Throw yourself into networking**—networking is the best way to advertise yourself because people don't just hear your message. When you're networking properly, they hear your message, see it in action, and feel the sincerity with which you deliver and live it (see chapter 4 for networking ideas and tips).

- **Surround yourself with the people you admire and those you want to become**—it's hard to build a "dedicated and tireless worker" brand when you're surrounded by lazy people, and it's almost impossible to build a "business leader" brand when you spend all your networking time with independent contractors who operate their one-person shops. So surround yourself with people you admire and who can add value to you and your brand even as you are doing the same for them. As much as possible, be with the people you want to become. If you want to be a leader, put yourself as close as possible to leaders. Learn from them and let them see your leadership qualities and your willingness to develop ever further.

- **Run your life like a business**—you can feel like you're stuck with many of the people in your life, including family, friends, fellow members of the church or clubs, and business associates. Some of them will be "off brand" for you, and continuing to associate with them will slow you down or maybe drag you under. So be the CEO of your life and feel free to "fire" the people slowing or dragging you down even if they're family members or old friends. Limit your contact with some of these people and cut it off entirely for others.

Then go on a "hiring spree," looking for great on-brand people to be your friends, employees, and others in your life.

- **Create goals and a timeline to meet them**—building your brand requires a lot of time and effort, and at least some money, so be strategic and efficient. Create some long-term goals for yourself, perhaps "serving on two key committees by next year." Then identify candidate committees, learn who is already on them, determine how to join, and figure out how you can add great value to each of the selected committees. Once you know your end goals, you can create clear and concise timelines to help you move forward. You can also set aside other brand-building activities not your priority at the moment. And you can break your end goals into smaller more manageable tasks, so you're not overwhelmed trying to do it all at once.

- **Always keep your end goal in mind**—building your brand is a long-term endeavor. Progress may be slow in the beginning, and you'll feel frustrated. Some of your plans will fail, and you won't meet certain goals. Your brand will evolve as you do, requiring more building efforts with each shift in the brand. And there's a fair chance that outside factors—such as a pandemic or major shift in your industry—will force you to rebuild your brand. That's all par for the course. Expect it, keep your eye on your goal, and keep moving forward.

When building and broadcasting your brand, always remember that this is not a popularity contest. Your brand won't appeal to everyone, and that's fine because you're not trying to attract everyone. The more specific and precise your brand is, the better because you'll be attracting exactly the people you want to work with.

A Quick Note on Aspirations

Some people have difficulty discovering their brand—that is, they don't really know what they are like. Perhaps they've been told that they're thus-and-such by their parents, teachers, or culture. Or maybe they've struggled through life and never given any thought to who they are.

If you're having trouble discovering your brand, think about what you aspire to do and to be one day—or *not* to do and *not* to be. When you're imagining this wonderful future, how do you see yourself? What are you thinking, saying, and doing? Ask yourself questions:

- What excites you when thinking about your future? What kind of person would you have to be to ensure that this future comes to be?
- What do you fear happening to you? And what do you have to become to prevent that?
- What's fun for you?
- What do you dislike?
- What people, jobs, or activities energize you?
- What people, jobs, or activities drain you?
- Who do you admire and why?
- Why do you disdain and why?

This list of questions doesn't come close to covering all the ways you can think about your future. But they point you in the right direction: In your heart of hearts, what great person do you aspire to be? And what does that person do and say? How does she live and relate to others?

Key Points

- Your personal brand is built upon who you truly are, what you value, and what value you bring to others and to organizations.
- Some people know what their brand is, while others have to discover it. A good way to discover your brand is to write your eulogy and see how you would like to be remembered. That tells you what you value and how you want to be seen—essential ingredients for your personal brand.
- You may not realize that you already have a brand, which consists of what people already think about you and say about you when you're not in the room. That brand may be exactly the brand you want and need, or you may have to work to change it.
- You can spread your brand by broadcasting it: acting in accordance with it, always showing up dressed for the role you want to have, always being prepared, being cognizant of the things you do and say, carefully considering the company you keep, sprinkling humble mentions of your brand in your conversation, and, in brief, being the living manifestation of your brand.
- You build your brand by thinking about the people you want to attract, honing your elevator pitch, throwing yourself into networking, surrounding yourself with the people you admire and want to become, running your life like a business, creating goals and a timeline to meet them, and always keeping your end goal in mind.

CHAPTER 4

Build a Network

Your network is your net worth.

—Porter Gale

||||||||||||||||||||||||||||||||||||||||||||||||||||||||

Even huge successes need people. Sheryl Sandberg turned to her mentor for advice and assistance at crucial points in her career. She became Facebook COO on her merits but freely acknowledges her mentor's importance.

Larry Page and Sergey Brin were the visionaries with the idea for a new kind of search engine, which they built on their own. But they needed that $100,000 check from investor Andy Bechtolsheim to turn Google into a viable company.

Tierra Kavanaugh Wayne had an idea for a diversity training and small-business consultancy. She already had a solid business background but needed assistance with interviews and other matters, so she turned to her mother. Together, they founded TKT & Associates, which, thirteen years later, was a $135 million company.

You are the one setting off on a great adventure; but to get to the starting point, you needed people to train you, equip you, supply you, and maybe finance you. Now you need people to help you pick the best route, deal with obstacles along the way, offer a helping hand when you stumble, and for many other reasons. You'll need people all along your journey, which is why networks are so important.

You Already Have a Network

Networking is the No. 1 unwritten rule of success in business.

—Sallie Krawcheck

||||||||||||||||||||||||||||||||||||||||||||||||||||||||||||

When we're starting out, many of us believe we don't have a network and can't possibly develop one. And it may be true that we have no connections in our industry, don't know any potential partners or suppliers, don't have a mentor, and don't even know how to go about contacting venture capitalists. Plus, we have little or no money of our own, so we can't create a network by flying from city to city to meet people at industry seminars and trade shows.

But everyone has some connections even if it's just with family members, some friends and work acquaintances, plus a couple of old classmates who would be happy to reconnect. The people in our little network may know absolutely nothing about our industry and have no background in business. But they could help out by listening as we practice our pitch or help us assemble the prototype, hand out flyers, or mind our booth at the local trade fair. They might also be our very first investors. Many successful entrepreneurs got their seed money from family members, and it does not require large amounts like the $100,000 that Edward Zuckerberg reportedly loaned to his son Mark[4] or the $245,000 that Mike and Jackie Bezos invested in

---

[4] Gene Marks, "Entrepreneurs are great, but it's mom and dad who gave them their start," *The Guardian* (January 31, 2021), accessed February 26, 2022, https://www.theguardian.com/business/2021/jan/31/small-business-entrepreneurs-success-parents.

their son Jeff's brand-new company, which was going to sell books on a new thing called the Internet.[5]

Many hugely successful companies were started with much less. Berry Gordy used the $700 he got from his father to create Motown Records, which poured out hit after hit. And Janice Bryant Howroyd combined the $900 she borrowed from her mother with $600 of her own to open what became the ActOne Group. That company grew to become the largest workforce management business owned by a woman and made Howroyd the first black woman to create and run a billion-dollar business.[6]

The tiniest network, consisting of just one person we already know, can be incredibly helpful. If nothing else, one other person who believes in us can give us the emotional boost we need to keep going—and that can be priceless.

We'll talk about expanding and utilizing your network soon. But first, let's look at the *net* and the *work* in *network*.

---

[5] Zameena Mejia, "Jeff Bezos got his parents to invest nearly $250,000 in Amazon in 1995 – they might be worth $30 billion today," *CNBC MakeIt* (August 2, 2018), accessed February 26, 2022, https://www.cnbc.com/2018/08/02/how-jeff-bezos-got-his-parents-to-invest-in-amazon--turning-them-into.html.

[6] Courtney Connley, "How Janice Bryant Howroyd turned a $900 loan from her mom into a billion-dollar business," *CNBC MakeIt* (April 20, 2018), accessed January 20, 2022, https://www.cnbc.com/2018/04/20/janice-bryant-howroyd-used-1500-to-start-a-billion-dollar-business.html.

The Net in Network

Networking is ... about connecting people with people,
people with ideas, and people with opportunities.

—Michele Jennae

Think of your network as being a fishing net you cast into the waters to find clients or customers, peers, partners, information, ideas, financing, potential employees, suppliers, and more. Your net should be large enough to bring in what you need but not so large that it's unwieldy or captures more than you can handle. It should be created with care, so it's robust and long-lasting. And it should be cast with discretion, or else, you'll waste time fishing in barren waters.

Imagine that you're in your workshop weaving your net. You already have the single-most-important strand for your net—you—and can quickly weave into that the few strands representing the small network you already have consisting of family members plus a few friends and old classmates. When you finish weaving that together, you have a small net. It's a tightly woven net, for you know everyone in the network personally and already spend a fair amount of time with each. You have a good relationship with everyone and have done favors for them in the past, so they're happy to help you out. And many of them already know each other, so ideas and information can spread rapidly through your little web.

It's a good, strong net, but it's limited. You'd like to make it bigger by weaving in more strands. As you do so, consider how large your net should be. You can acquire lots of new strands to weave in by meeting people at mixers, industry seminars, trade shows, church, and social gatherings. But how many events can you attend? How many new names can you take and do something with as opposed to tossing them into a drawer and never following up? It doesn't do you any good to meet potential clients, suppliers, partners, and others if you can't get back to them soon with interesting ideas, well-crafted proposals, or specific requests. In fact, it may do you harm by giving you a reputation for not being serious. That's why it's better to have a smaller net you can handle with skill rather than a larger net you struggle with. Your net will grow with time as you interact with more and more people. But it should never be so large that you cannot handle it, that you leave most of what you catch to rot.

You must also think carefully about the creation and maintenance of your net. Imagine a real fishing net woven together from various bits of rope, plastic, belts, and suspenders, plus paperclips strung together. That net will begin to fray almost immediately, and the fisherman will spend countless hours maintaining and repairing it only to see it fall apart again. So when weaving your net, think carefully about every strand before including it. Weak strands do you no good; neither do strands that are inconsistent with the others. They make your net unwieldy and inefficient and take the place of other strands that would make the net stronger.

Do you really want to spend time and resources weaving in net strands that don't do you much good, like the five thousand LinkedIn contacts you've collected but never developed relationships with? Sure, you send them your posts and hit them with requests to like your page or watch your video seminar, but are these strands worth the time and effort to maintain and cultivate them? If you're not actively working to maintain strands in your net, they're making your net overly big, unwieldy, and ultimately weak.

Finally, your net should be cast with discretion. Casting it willy-nilly may bring in some results, but are they the results you need? You might be looking for a specific catch or different catches at different times. Early on, you may hope to net anybody who can be helpful in any way. Later, perhaps after you're established relationships with a mentor and the financial folks, you may only want to fish for suppliers and partners. Still later, when your company is large and secure, you may cast your net for peers, industry leaders, and government officials.

You always want to cast your net in the appropriate waters; and since your needs will evolve, you must always consider where you are fishing, why you are fishing there, and whether there is a better place to fish.

If you build, maintain, and cast your net with care, you'll reap the rewards. And always remember that your net has a special feature that a real fishnet doesn't. That special feature is you—the strand at the very center, the heart of your net. You have something valuable to offer to the contacts, clients, referrals, peers, partners, information, ideas, financing, potential employees, suppliers, and others your net touches. If you handle the *you* part of your net properly, people will be happy to be "caught" in your network.

The Work *in Network*

We've all seen it: the breathtaking way some guy sweeps his way through a networking event, trade show, or other gatherings. He's got a big smile on his face, strides right up to strangers, shakes their hands, gives his pitch, hands them his card and brochure, and moves on to the next. He powers through the room in no time, working it with confidence and precision, leaving with a thick handful of business cards and a big smile of success on his face. He's sure that he's the master of networking. But the people he thinks he's "captured" never got into his net. And if they did, they'll wriggle out in no time and make sure they're never caught again.

He thinks he's worked hard and will reap the rewards. But the reality is he just laid his net on the water for a few moments and then drew it back, empty except for the metaphorical equivalent of leaves and plastic wrappers floating on the surface. He hasn't worked at networking at all.

The simple truth is that if you won't work at networking,

networking won't work for you. If you rush into an event after it has begun, run from person to person giving your pitch and shoving your business card into their hands, then leave. You haven't networked because you haven't worked.

Networking is work. You have to *work* at finding the right places to network, *work* at understanding the needs of the people who you will meet, *work* at learning to introduce yourself in a brief and informative manner, *work* at mastering the art of drawing people out in conversation, *work* at being a good listener, *work* at remaining in touch with and helping the people you meet, *work* at understanding and possibly implementing things you have learned from the people you have met, and *work* at following up on the leads you develop.

If you don't work at networking, and work hard, your network will be like a fishing net that's just sitting in the corner gathering dust: worthless!

And there's more to the *work* part of networking. Whether you're a leader, entrepreneur, or employee, you have to shine at what you do. You have to be so good that people in your network can't help but notice you and like what they see. That's when your network starts working for you. That's when people start referring potential clients, partners, or employees to you. That's when they hire, promote, or support you. That's when they connect you with others who help you in some way.

Many employees have risen through the ranks without ever interviewing for a job. That's because others in their network saw their potential and responded by promoting them or taking them with them when they moved up. Many entrepreneurs never had to look for clients or potential partners, thanks to referrals. If you work hard at creating a network of people looking at you and work hard at what you do, you may find doors opening before you even knock on them.

Network with Head Held High

One of the most powerful networking practices is to provide immediate value to a new connection.
This means the moment you identify a way to help someone, take action.

—Lewis Howes

|||||||||||||||||||||||||||||||||||||||||||||||||||||||||||||||

A lot of very smart and talented people are terrified by the idea of networking, especially of having to walk into a room full of strangers and give pitch after pitch. I've been to more networking opportunities than I can count over the past fifteen years, so I can tell that networking is *not* about endless pitching. It's not about bending anyone's ears or struggling to get people to listen to your memorized speech.

Networking is letting people know what you have to offer and being so good at what you do that they cannot help but ask to learn more. And they will! No matter how small your company may be, no matter what product or service you offer, or no matter how low you are on the company ladder, you have something that somebody needs. You can get something done for them; you can solve their problem. And you really can solve their problem because you shine at what you do. So don't go into networking events with hat in hand, hoping someone will be willing to listen to your pitch. Go in with the certainty that you have something that someone needs. It's just a matter of finding them or finding someone who knows them and can connect with you.

You may have to go to many events and meet many people to find those someones. You may have to refine your offering several times, and you may have to work hard to improve your listening and helping skills. But success is inevitable if you understand the *net* and *work* parts of networking and realize that people really do want to meet you, talk to you, and work with you. It's just a matter of time and opportunity.

And always remember that only thinking about what your network can do for you is the best way to bring it all to a crashing halt. Instead, always be thinking about what you can do for others, what introductions you can make, what information you can pass on, and how you can help someone in any way. The more helpful you are, the more people will be willing to help you in return. And these need not be one-for-one exchanges, as in "I'll help you just so you'll help me in equal measure." Help others generously without expecting anything in return. In so doing, you'll make yourself more valuable and will shine all the more brightly. In other words, we eventually reap the harvest that we have sown.

One Size Does Not Fit All

Your networking needs will be different from everyone else's because of your specific business or employment goals, financial resources, existing contacts, and other factors.

If you're opening a local business, such as a hair salon or chiropractic office, a "neighborhood networking" focus may fulfill most of your needs. In the very beginning, when you're hoping to get that first client and you need a logo and a little space to rent, local people can be helpful. Networking through the nearby Chamber of Commerce or Rotary Club and at church and charity functions might put you in touch with a local real estate agent who knows of offices for rent, a designer who can whip up some marketing materials, and some potential clients/customers.

Since most of your customers will be found within a five- or ten-mile radius of your physical location, a "neighborhood networking" focus may be just right for you forever. Flying around the country to attend regional and national industry conferences probably won't get you many more clients or customers. It would, however, still be worthwhile to go to some of these events, for you can learn and meet peers with whom you can swap ideas and lessons. But for the most part, you're best off casting your net in local waters. And as you meet more people and learn more about the services in your neighborhood, you can be even more helpful to the other people in your network.

If, on the other hand, you're opening a business like mine, which supplies services to federal government agencies, a partnership-focused networking effort makes more sense. The second iteration of my business—the one I invented on the spot at a seminar that I discuss in more detail in chapter 6—flew off the ground because of a partnership that came from introducing myself to the people at my seminar table. With a partnership-focused business, neighborhood networking events are not terribly useful. Instead, it makes sense to cast your net at seminars, trade shows, and other events geared toward your industry.

At these larger events, you might be able to chat with potential partners sitting at your table or at an event mixer. But to get to certain people, you may have to schedule an appointment to meet with them at the event, which means your networking begins long before the event opens. If that's the case, networking for a single event can be a long-term process as you think about who you want to connect with at an upcoming event, check with your existing contacts to see if anyone can make an introduction or advise you on how to get one, and prepare ideas and materials specific to the person you want to meet before arriving at the event.

So think carefully before rushing off to any old networking event. Yes, you never know where you'll find that person or piece of information that takes you to the next level. But for the most part, you're best off looking for the people and things you need in the places where they are most likely to be found.

One Size Doesn't Even Fit You!

It's important to spend time thinking about what you hope to catch with your networking. At various times, you may be looking for the following:

- Advisors who can take a bird's-eye view of your situation and offer guidance
- Experts who can offer assistance in specific situations
- Customers or clients
- Financing
- Key employees
- Mentors
- Outside services, perhaps accounting and marketing
- Partners
- Peers to share with and learn from
- Suppliers

You might need many or all these people and services at some point. But what do you need now to take your next step forward? Where are you likely to find what you need? How do the people you need to meet like to be contacted, and what information do they want from you? Yes, people and offers sometimes come in out of the blue, and you have to scramble to prepare to meet them. But most of the time, you'll meet the people you've been looking for, so think carefully about where you cast your net.

And let your networking efforts evolve as you do. Bear in mind that the type of people you were hoping to meet last year may not be the same as those you're hoping to meet today. You may have had a great time and made wonderful friends networking at the local Chamber of Commerce, but if your business has shifted beyond your neighborhood, your networking efforts must shift as well. That's not to say that you should ruthlessly cull through your net and dump everyone not helpful today. But be willing to shift your networking efforts over time. Honor and respect those contacts you've already made but never hesitate to fish in new waters as your needs evolve.

And while you're thinking about your present networking needs, ask yourself what you will be needing over the long run, so you can start preparing for it now.

Where and How to Network

Networking is not a discreet activity carried on at specific places. That is, you don't network from nine to five at work or between 7:30 p.m. and 9:30 pm at the industry conference mixer. The best networkers are always prepared to meet new people, share what they do, exchange information and ideas, and help others out.

That being said, there are many unassuming places to network:

- Chambers of Commerce, churches, and other neighborhood venues. Even if they're not specifically designed as networking activities, they put you in contact with other people.
- Associations in your field
- Conferences, seminars, and trade shows in your field
- LinkedIn and other social networking sites
- Sororities or fraternities
- Your child's Little League soccer or football games
- On an airplane
- Hair salons or barbershops
- Social gatherings
- Fundraisers
- Golf and tennis courses
- Dog parks
- The gym

Be sure to include key figures on YouTube and other podcasting sites in your networking efforts. It's true that you don't really meet these people and that the flow of information is one-way only, but many sites offer great information from bona fide experts. It's also possible to initiate relationships by offering intelligent, well-thought-out comments.

When networking, whether in person or virtually, look for people who are aligned with your goals and hang in those clusters. Join the appropriate organizations and be present, be seen, be on committees, and always offer value. As mentioned previously in the chapter on branding, become the person whose name is mentioned even when you're not in the room because you are such a shining star. Develop a reputation for helping others, for being hardworking, or other qualities so powerfully, so clearly, that your reputation supersedes.

Networking is so important because it's a great way to become known and trusted. We like to buy from people we know and trust. We can Google for products and services and find a list of companies that provide them, but we prefer to buy from someone we know and trust. Or from someone recommended by someone else we know and trust.

Then again, there are times when networking by Googling and cold-calling will give great results. When I first began IFAS, I went through the lists of government contracts being awarded to identify the contact person for each. My idea was to reach out to each of these contacts to see if their companies would work with me, if not with this particular contract, then perhaps with another project. I had already been successful with subcontracting army work, so I cold-called and sent emails to these contacts. Someone from a midsized business called me back, so I gave him my pitch.

He said, "How did you know what we were looking for?"

I had no idea what he was talking about.

He continued, "We have been directed by the government

agency to bring on subcontractors to a specific project that fits your company's profile as a small minority woman- and veteran-owned firm."

Great! I got a subcontract with them and was able to put ten people on that project, all from Googling contract lists and cold-calling. They mentored me, and when I was growing at a pace I couldn't keep up with, they also helped me financially. Usually, at various points in a contract, you send in an invoice and wait thirty to forty-five days for payment. Having to wait that long for money when I first started the company was very difficult for me. However, once I created the invoice on my computer and hit Send, within five minutes, I'd call and ask if it was okay for me to come and pick up the check. Physically. My contact would say, "Sure, I'll put it at the front desk for you."

They didn't have to do that for me. They could have made me wait for one, two, even three months to get the check. But the company leaders became those special people in my network who helped me along the way.

One year, the same company nominated my company, IFAS, for the United States Small Business Administration's Subcontractor of the Year Award. Although we didn't win the award, the nomination from a firm that I had grown to respect and admire meant a lot.

A Note on Networking within a Company

You can make more friends in two months by becoming
interested in other people than you can in two years by
trying to get other people interested in you.

—Dale Carnegie

||||||||||||||||||||||||||||||||||||||||||||||||||||||||||

The principles of networking are the same for employees looking to move up as they are for entrepreneurs. That is, begin with the contacts you already have even if it's just two people in your department and someone you've kept up with from your old position in a different location. Make your net large enough to bring in what you need but not so large that it's unwieldy or captures more than you can handle. Create your net with care so it's robust, and cast it with discretion.

You can easily network with people in your area and those you meet at company functions. You can also reach out to others but do so carefully. Simply asking a higher-up in a different team, department, or location for promotion won't be helpful. But you can, for example, ask if you can have fifteen minutes of their time to learn about something they are doing well so that you can share the knowledge with your team or department. Show up to the session prepared, ask intelligent questions, and follow up with a thank-you note or a summary of how you've implemented what you learned. This can make quite an impression.

If you've recently completed a course or earned a new certification, think about who in your company can use what you know for a specific project and ask to be included on the team. This would only be a temporary position, but it would give you an opportunity to display your excellence to another leader who may become a mentor, promote you, or recommend you to others.

The key thing about networking with leaders within a company is to demonstrate that you are vitally interested in the company, are eager to learn more or share what you have learned, and are willing to work hard. To put yourself in contact with people who can help, attend company seminars, programs, and outings; ask to be assigned to intra- and interdepartmental projects; reach out and congratulate others when they get a promotion or otherwise deserve recognition; introduce people when you think they might be able to help each other; be open to connecting with the people you meet in shared spaces and otherwise put yourself out there in a positive and helpful manner.

And never forget the importance of networking outside of your company even if you wish to move up within your company. Oftentimes, you have to move out to move up—that is, switch to a different company to get the promotion. So even if your heart is set on moving up the ladder in the company where you are currently working, be prepared to move out, so you can move up and maybe return to your original company at a higher level later.

Key Points

- P²D is essential to leaders and leaders-to-be, but no one goes all the way as a one-person team. We all need people. We need a network of people.
- Networking does not mean finding people you can use and then dropping. Networking is about finding people in the industry or sector who can bring value to you and, just as importantly, whom you are willing to bring value to in return.
- Building a "net" with care means carefully considering who you want to "catch." Otherwise, your net will become too big and unwieldy.
- Neglecting the "work" part of networking means leaving your net to go to waste.

- Networking is an art. It requires finding the right places to network, understanding the needs of the people you will meet, learning to introduce yourself, mastering the art of drawing people out in conversation and being a good listener, staying in touch with the people you meet, understanding what they have learned, and following up on the leads you developed.

CHAPTER 5

Be Intentional

*Intentional living is the art of making our own choices
before others' choices make us.*

—Richie Norton

|||||||||||||||||||||||||||||||||||||||||||||||||||||

Barbara Corcoran, the Queen of New York Real Estate and one
of the sharks on TV's *Shark Tank*, is fiercely intentional. But she
certainly wasn't on the fast track to success when she began in
the working world. By age twenty-three, she had bounced with
dizzying speed from job to job—a total of twenty that included
selling books, serving as an orphanage housemother, peddling hot
dogs, waitressing, and being a receptionist for a real estate company.

It was while waitressing that she met and began dating an older
man who was a builder. She had long wanted to be her own boss,
so together, they opened an apartment-rental agency in Manhattan.
Soon enough, they had fourteen agents working under them. But
then disaster struck: her boyfriend announced that he was marrying
one of their secretaries. Their company soon split up, Barbara was on
her own, and she swore to herself that she would never fail again. She
was so determined to do whatever it took that when her company
was in serious financial trouble—and $400,000 in debt—she left
her real estate business in the hands of a trusted subordinate and
took a full-time job that she despised to earn enough to keep her
real estate business alive.

Barbara had other strong intentions, such as never letting men
talk down to her. Back then, even though the majority of residential

real estate agents in New York were women, it was the men who controlled the industry as owners, developers, and financiers. Some felt that it was their right to talk down to the women who worked for them, but Barbara refused to accept it. She had seen her father talk down to her mother too many times and commented that "even as a little kid, I said to myself I would never, ever, let a man speak to me like that. It lit a fuse inside of me."[7]

That wasn't the only intention fueling her success. Born dyslexic, she had struggled in school and was bullied by teachers and classmates, who called her dumb. She responded by deciding that she would prove them wrong. "I worked harder than anyone to overcome my 'weakness,' and it's a large part of my success."[8]

How is her success measured? In 2001, she sold her real estate firm for $66 million and has since enjoyed a very successful career as an author, speaker, and, of course, a shark.

As Corcoran's story shows, being intentional is a key factor in the success equation. Being intentional means developing a strong vision of what we want and then focusing on the things that matter. We must focus on the big things we want to achieve, as well as on the smaller things that take us one step closer toward our passion. Being intentional means pushing aside the distractions, no matter how enticing or entertaining, and keeping both eyes firmly fixed on the goal. It means forging ahead even when we have to delay or sacrifice something else—even if we have to get a full-time job we don't like to keep our dream alive. Being intentional can be difficult,

---

[7] Kris Frieswick, "Why Barbara Corcoran Thinks Growing Up Poor Is a Key Ingredient for Success." *Inc.* (November 2016), accessed January 3, 2022, https://www.inc.com/magazine/201611/kris-frieswick/barara-corcoran-beyond-shark-tank.html.

[8] Taylor Locke, "Barbara Corcoran: How dyslexia 'made me a millionaire,'" *CNBC MakeIt* (March 10, 2020), accessed January 3, 2022, https://www.cnbc.com/2020/03/10/barbara-corcoran-how-dyslexia-made-me-a-millionaire.html.

but it brings all our resources to bear on the goal. It also makes us shine and turns us into a star. Others see our efforts and are drawn to us. These people become our friends, guides, mentors, and "door openers," helping us to advance ever further.

Being intentional does not mean giving things up. Being intentional means understanding what really matters and then tirelessly, relentlessly, fearlessly focusing on what is necessary to turn the dream into reality.

We don't always know if we will succeed in any particular endeavor, for there are many factors in life we cannot control. But by being intentional, we declare to ourselves and others that we will not be distracted by the frivolous or deterred by the difficult or dismayed by setbacks. We are telling the world that we are determined to succeed.

What Are We Saying?

You are what you do, not what you say you'll do.
—C. G. Jung

|||||||||||||||||||||||||||||||||||||||||||||||||||||

People have all kinds of goals—from getting the next promotion to launching a startup that will revolutionize the world. Everything begins as an idea, a concept, a notion; but many of us go no further than the dreaming and talking stages. Why? Because we're not intentional. We're not devoting all our time, energy, and resources to succeeding. And we don't realize that we're broadcasting our lack of intentionality loudly and clearly.

Think about it. What are we saying when we

- Spend several hours a day on social media?
- Skip the networking meeting because we're too tired to go?
- Keep finding household projects that "just must be done"?
- Hang with friends or go to the party rather than practice the presentation that we must soon make to the board?
- Decide that earning the necessary certificate or degree will cut too deeply into our sleep time or fun time?
- Bury ourselves in endless details and duties that should be handled by someone else?

When we do things like these, we're saying that we're not really serious about our goal or that it's not a true passion.

Suppose we continue renting that large apartment rather than move in with friends or parents. Or decline to swap the luxury SUV for a more economical sedan. Or in any other way give up what we really could do without rather than invest in our passion.

Suppose we cling to relationships with people who do not share our vision. Who entices us away from what we really need to be doing, who doubts or even mocks our goals, or who undermines our confidence?

Suppose we find ourselves stressing over a business plan that never seems good enough. Or spending so much time chasing after certificates and degrees that we lose sight of our primary objective. Or finding excuse after excuse to not ask for the financing or other support we need.

When we're caught in situations like these, when we're doing things that distract from our passion, or when we're unable to decide what is the most important thing to do next, we're telling ourselves that we're not absolutely clear about the goal. That's when we have to ask ourselves: What really matters? What is most important? What are we willing to be absolutely intentional about?

It's important that we answer these questions with brutal honesty, for it is only when we are clear about the goal that we can take the difficult steps necessary. And difficult steps will always be necessary.

Intentionality Is Much More than Time

It's choice—not chance—that determines your destiny.
—Jean Nidetch

‖‖‖‖‖‖‖‖‖‖‖‖‖‖‖‖‖‖‖‖‖‖‖‖‖‖‖‖‖‖‖‖‖‖‖‖‖‖

Some people are very clear about the goal but confuse being intentional with putting in time. They feel that if they just spend enough time on something, all will be well. Whether they know it or not, they're influenced by the ten-thousand-hour rule—the idea that if they devote a tremendous amount of time to mastering a certain topic or skill set, they will be among the very best at it. If you don't put the time in, you might be good, but you won't be great.

This idea arose from research conducted in the 1990s that looked at top-flight musicians and found there was a direct link between time spent practicing and success. The concept became popularized as the idea that success was a matter of putting your nose to the grindstone and leaving it there for years. But later research showed that while time was important, it wasn't the only factor. How you used your time was just as important. Simply playing the same musical pieces over and over, for example, wasn't as productive as getting good coaching, identifying your weaknesses, and other factors—and then practicing some more.

The lesson for us is that we must be intentional with our time. We must be smart and self-aware, as humble about our abilities as we are bold in our dreams, and as willing to make course corrections as we are determined to succeed. We must know what we want and then arrange matters so that we can devote all the resources necessary to achieve that goal. These resources include our time, energy, wisdom, financial resources, mentors, colleagues, and contacts.

Think of being intentional as packing for a long trek over high mountains. We'll only have what we can carry in our backpack, so we must be sure to take everything we need. But since everything we take must be carried on our back, we'll have to pack as lightly as possible.

What do we need to be intentional? What key items must we pack for our trek to success?

- **Time**—the backpack must be stuffed with as much time as possible, for success is a long journey. It took Thomas Edison a thousand tries to invent the lightbulb. Howard Schultz was turned down more than two hundred times when he sought financing for his Starbucks idea. Milton Hershey saw three of his candy companies fail before finding success. Walt Disney's first company, Laugh-O-Gram, failed; and his first successful character, Oswald the Rabbit, was stolen away from him by competitors. Yes, some people are overnight successes, but they are very few and far between. If we aren't prepared for a long journey to success, we'll drop out before reaching the goal.
- **Determination to improve**—no matter how knowledgeable, experienced, and skilled we may be, we will have to learn and grow along the way. The terrain will be more difficult than we had imagined, and there will be unfamiliar obstacles to overcome. We must pack a good supply of determination to improve, or else, we will give up.
- **Awareness of what we are doing**—it is easy to get lost along the way, waste time wandering down the wrong trails, become completely turned around, get caught in a landslide, and maybe even fall off a cliff. Awareness of what we are doing serves as our compass for the journey.
- **Ability to push past errors**—everyone makes mistakes, so we can expect to get off course on the trek to success. It took James Dyson fifteen years and over five thousand prototypes to develop his bag-less vacuum cleaner. Richard Branson dropped out of high school and served time in

jail for publishing forbidden material in the magazine that was his first business enterprise before Virgin Airlines. And even after he tasted success, he still failed with Virgin Cola, Virgin Vodka, Virgin Clothing, Virgin Digital, and others. Everyone fails. What matters is what we do after the big mistake. What's important is how we absorb the lessons learned and avoid the same errors in the future.

- **Willingness to tackle those tasks we don't want to—** everyone is happy to trek on even ground, but what happens when the path becomes steep, or we have to haul ourselves up the side of a cliff? We may not like rough roads, but we can be sure there will be more than a few on the journey to success.

- **Ability to ask for help**—even the most experienced trekkers rely on friends and guides to help them through the journey, especially when the path becomes difficult. If we can't ask for help, we're liable to find ourselves falling off the cliff. No matter how much of an expert we are in our field, we can use help. Steve Jobs and Steve Wozniak may have been computer and marketing geniuses, but they brought in an experienced businessman to serve as the first CEO of Apple.

- **Good physical health and energy**—expect there to be many impossibly long days, nights without sleep, marathon meetings or manufacturing sessions, endless disappointments, and more exhausting activities. We need to pack plenty of good health and energy in the form of healthful eating, time carved out to rest, helpful practices such as meditation or yoga, and whatever else is needed to stay in tip-top shape.

- **Good mental health**—there's an excellent chance that we'll take many falls along the way, spend freezing nights out in the rain, go hungry, be chased by angry animals, and otherwise face adversity along the way. So we need to pack some mental health boosters—whether they be inspiring books to read, music or podcasts on our phone or pad, or whatever else that lifts the spirits.

- **Ability to celebrate success along the way**—the wise trekker stops to enjoy the scenery along the way and to celebrate the fact that they climbed a steep cliff, logged a certain number of miles today, or otherwise accomplished something wonderful. Likewise, we should celebrate our small wins along the road to success. We must applaud ourselves when we get that big client, hire our first or hundredth employee, open up a new line, get a new license or certification, get a promotion or bonus, or otherwise take a step forward on the journey.

Now that we've filled our bag with the items we need to succeed, let's look at how to use some of them: building your talents and skill sets, building relationships, and tamping down stress.

Intentionally Build Your Talents and Skillset

We cannot become what we need to be by remaining what we are.

—Max De Pree

||||||||||||||||||||||||||||||||||||||||||||||||||||

I can honestly say that formal education gave me book knowledge and a few degrees. However, getting informal education; growing up in St. Louis, Missouri; and serving in the army took that further by opening my eyes. They intensified my growth mindset and gave me the experience, wisdom, and intestinal fortitude to face challenging situations.

While in the U.S. Army, I served as an enlisted logistician and then later was commissioned as a finance officer. I was also in potentially explosive situations on more than a few occasions. I learned a lot from my duties, and I grew quite a bit from the whole experience. Without realizing it, I had invested a lot of time and effort into building skills I could capitalize on in the private sector and developing a toughness I could also take with me.

Identifying such transferable skills is invaluable—whether you gained these skills as part of the military, as a volunteer coach, as a teacher or coordinator, or in any other way. You already have them; you just have to leverage and use them. Even negative experiences can be learning experiences. Growing up in a disadvantaged or poverty-stricken home may have taught you how to be resourceful and resilient. Failing to make the cut for the high school basketball team may have taught you about determination and perseverance as you practiced for months and made the team the next year. Literally being laughed out of the room when you made a formal presentation or sang a song at an open mic event may have taught you that what seems like a total disaster is just another bump in the road.

Think of all your losses as lessons throughout life and use them to your advantage. And remember that obstacles are good. They're speed bumps that force us to slow down and live in the moment by dealing with things that require our full attention.

Reach deep within to identify and leverage all the knowledge, skills, and talents you already have. Then look to expand and grow some more. On the formal education side, you can enroll in seminars, college classes, in-service training, continuing education courses, and more. You can study simply to learn more, or you can go for new degrees and certificates. You can also study on your own by reading books, going to or downloading lectures on your computer, following great educators on social media, and other ways. You can join discussion groups in your field and learn from others.

As you learn, grow, and improve your skillset, whether formally or informally, you become better able to take on new tasks. You become stronger and more confident, which allows you to radiate confidence and optimism as you speak and work with others—even when you're asking them for a promotion, money, or something else.

Intentionally Build Relationships

Some people believe they can succeed entirely on their own. They think they'll invent a better product, and the world will flock to their door. They'll put up a fabulous website and watch the orders fly in, or they'll write a business proposal, and the money folks will compete to give them millions.

It rarely happens like this. The solo entrepreneur or lone genius is so rare as to be almost a myth. The truth is that you need people in key positions to succeed. You need friends to share good times with and friends who will listen to and applaud your dreams. You need coworkers and peers to exchange ideas with and to learn from. You need people working under you who will speak the truth to you and will do what they say they will do. You need teachers to educate you and possibly open doors for you. You need no-nonsense mentors who take a strong interest in you and tell you exactly what you need to hear, learn, and master. You need people who inspire you and people whom you may never meet but still thrill you with their stories of success and words of wisdom.

You need people—lots of them. They give you the information you lack, do the things you cannot, energize you, help you relax with your hobbies, and share the fun when you're at play. And of course, you need special people, your loved ones, who can be a tremendous source of happiness and motivation.

So work on your relationships at all levels. For your loved ones, hold them dear even as you acknowledge that you'll have less time to spend with them. Look for creative ways to work around the time crunch. It can be hard to come up with workarounds, but they're well worth the effort.

For your friends, let them know that while you are busy and have less time to spend with them while you're pursuing your dream, you cherish the good times you've shared together and look forward to more.

For coworkers and peers, give them all the dedication to the shared task that you would like for *them* to give. Come to all work sessions well prepared, optimistic, and ready to work. Support them with the same energy and enthusiasm that you would like for them to offer you. It's true that doing so is good for everyone. But it's even better for you because it makes you a standout. Key people will notice your energy, optimism, and commitment and will like what they see.

For the people working under you, be the boss you've always wanted to have. The supportive boss who leads by example helps people succeed by clearing away obstacles, and, while not allowing anyone to slack on their duties, practices firmness and fairness.

For your teachers and mentors, show them the respect they deserve by arriving at classes and one-on-one sessions well prepared, ears wide open, and eager to learn and improve. You don't have to agree with everything they say or suggest but treat what they say with the utmost respect. Don't hesitate to ask questions and push back a little; they'll probably enjoy the give and take with an interested, well-prepared student/mentee.

Intentionally Keep Your Stress Down

Working to get and stay ahead can be very stressful physically, mentally, and emotionally. Stress can cause headaches, muscle tension and pain, anxiety, outbursts of anger, social withdrawal, fatigue, problems sleeping, and more. But how do you reduce stress when the very thing you are doing is the source of your stress?

Those of us with a growth mindset don't want to stop pushing to get ahead, but this doesn't mean we just have to accept stress and its negative effects. Instead, we can add stress-reducing techniques to the mix. These include well-known stress-reducers:

- **Meditation**—the goal of meditation is to declutter the mind of the many thoughts competing for your attention even if only for a few minutes. This produces a sense of calm and balance and reduces stress. Meditation also helps one reduce negative emotions, focus on the present, develop a new perspective on a stressful situation, and come up with creative solutions. It may also help reduce anxiety, depression, headaches, and sleeping problems.

  An ancient practice, meditation is an easy, inexpensive tool that doesn't require extensive training or special equipment. You can meditate at your desk for a few minutes while at work or for lengthy periods at home. You can meditate by yourself or with others in a class or group. Arianna Huffington, the creator of the *Huff Post*, sets aside twenty to thirty minutes to meditate in the morning. She says that meditation is a powerful tool for improving performance and productivity. Oprah Winfrey, Panda Express founder Andrew Cherng, and Elements Truffles cofounder Alak Vasa are among the many other high achievers who meditate.

- **Yoga**—we tend to think of getting flexible when thinking of yoga, but there's more to it than that. Yoga practice incorporates breath control and meditation, which means it can help reduce stress even as it improves your ability to flex and use your body to overcome the aches and pains associated with busy business lives. I am told that yoga can also help you sleep better, which means you'll have more energy, better focus, and a brighter mood.

- **Religious faith**—various studies have shown that having religious faith can help reduce stress. Setting aside the specifics of the faith, the mere fact of believing in a higher power and belonging to a community of like-minded people can help reduce levels of fatigue, anxiety, and depression; improve coping skills, and strengthen the sense that life has meaning. An interesting study conducted by researchers from Baylor University found that faith and entrepreneurship are related. The researchers found that "American entrepreneurs pray more frequently, are more likely to see God as personal, and are more likely to attend services in congregations that encourage business and profit-making."[9] I firmly believe that without my faith in God, I would've thrown in the towel a long time ago when building my business. "Faith it until you make it" rather than "fake it until you make it" was how I got by.

- **Hobbies**—Marissa Mayer, the former Yahoo CEO, bakes for fun. "My hobbies actually make me better at work,"

---

[9] Baylor University, "Entrepreneurs Pray More, See God as Personal, Baylor Researchers Find," (Baylor University: June 4, 2013), accessed January 6, 2022, https://www.baylor.edu/mediacommunications/news.php?action=story&story=130615.

she says. "They help me come up with new and innovative ways of looking at things."[10] Richard Branson's hobby is playing chess. For him, "it combines the greatest aspects of many different sports—tactics, planning, bravery, and risk-taking—plus you can have a cup of tea and often a stimulating conversation while you play."[11] There are endless varieties of hobbies. Michelle Obama runs, while Condoleezza Rice golfs. Bill Gates plays bridge and tennis. Tom Hanks collects old-fashioned typewriters. Anna Wintour plays tennis early in the morning before heading into her offices at *Vogue*, where she serves as editor in chief. As for me, I recharge my batteries by traveling to get a change of scenery. What you do for a hobby isn't as important as that it refreshes your mind and reduces stress.

Then there are lesser-known methods of reducing stress:

- **Learn to say no**—*no* is a difficult word for many of us to utter, for we've been taught to be nice to other people. We may even have been told that it's our duty to help others, especially family members and friends. While it's wonderful to assist others, we have to remember that a *yes* is likely to pull us away from our main focus and make our lives more difficult, and more stressful. We have to remember that we can't be all things to all people, and by focusing our efforts on success now, we can help more people later.
- **Declutter your life**—pursuing the passion demands that we devote as much time, focus, and energy as possible to the goal. We can't do that when our desks, schedules, homes,

---

[10] Hilary Hoffower and Marguerite Ward, "22 hobbies of highly successful people," *Insider* (August 5, 2020), accessed January 6, 2022, https://www.businessinsider.com/hobbies-successful-people-2017-2.

[11] Ibid.

and lives are crammed with extraneous stuff. We need to clear unnecessary papers from our desks, unnecessary tasks and meetings from our schedules, and unnecessary stuff from our homes. Literally throwing things away is often a great approach. If that's too difficult, we can box them up and stow 'em away.

We must also remove unnecessary people from our lives. If that seems coldhearted, think of it this way: The people you need in your life right now are those who love you, support you, teach you, mentor you, train you, and otherwise help you improve. Anybody who is *not* doing one of these things is holding you back.

Shedding the people, items, and tasks holding us back takes a huge load off our shoulders and reduces stress. When the only things in our lives are those we really need, really like, or otherwise make our lives more fulfilling, everything we do is productive, fun, or both.

- **Eliminate bad habits**—bad habits are not only time wasters but are also stress builders. Overindulging in alcohol or drugs means we'll be less productive at work, which will lead to failures and stress. Being chronically late will anger our coworkers, bosses, and potential investors, which leads to stress. Procrastinating, stretching ourselves too thin, being disorganized, fearing change, blaming others for our mistakes—every bad habit you can think of interferes with our productivity, enjoyment, or both. This means that every bad habit makes us more stressed.

Reducing stress with any of these methods is a great investment. And if you use two or more methods, your returns will increase exponentially.

Are You Intentional or Just Busy?

Never confuse movement with action.

—Ernest Hemingway

||||||||||||||||||||||||||||||||||||||||||||||||||

How can we tell if we're being intentional or just burying ourselves in busy work that doesn't move us toward the goal? Think about these things:

- **Enjoying**—are you keeping up with all your hobbies, concerts, athletic activities, and what have you? Do you feel as if you really haven't had to give up a lot of fun time?
- **Clinging**—have you kept all your relationships intact with all your family members, close friends, acquaintances, neighbors, social media friends, and so on?
- **Undermining**—are you still spending time with people who don't share or support your dream? Even if the time is only virtual by way of texts?
- **Distracting**—do you still have all those fun but time-wasting apps on your phone and computer?
- **Wavering**—are you still unsure about your priorities? About what you should and should not be doing to meet your goal?
- **Ambling**—do you decide what to do at the spur of the moment rather than figuring out ahead of time which tasks are high priority and which are not?
- **Controlling**—are you doing things that could be done by employees, trusted outside contractors, or advisors? Are you micromanaging every aspect of your business?
- **Fretting**—are you spending a lot of time worrying when you could be working?
- **Declining**—are you ignoring your mentor's guidance and otherwise turning down advice and instruction because

you believe that you, and only you, truly understand the situation? Are you refusing to receive emotional support when you're down?

- **Yessing**—are you saying yes to every request for your time and energy even when you know that what you're being asked to do will take you away from what you need to do?
- **Idling**—do you find yourself with idle time on your hands perhaps while you're waiting for the next appointment or sitting in the doctor's waiting room? Have you got nothing to do because you didn't bring along a book or a pen and pad? Or didn't download a phone app that will allow you to be productive while waiting around?
- **Skipping**—are you passing up opportunities to meet potentially helpful people, learn something, or introduce yourself and your company/service to people?
- **Organizing**—do you find that you simply must do a lot of things before you can settle into work, such as carefully reading all the messages in your spam folder just to make sure they're really spam?
- **Staying in the comfort zone**—are you happy to handle all your tasks and duties? Is there nothing that makes you hesitate or wish that someone else would do?
- **Zipping through**—do you find that you often finish your day early and have plenty of idle time on your hands? Do you wish you could think of something else to do to move forward to your goal?

If you can answer yes to more than a few of the questions above, you're not being nearly intentional enough. Or maybe not intentional at all.

American philosopher Henry David Thoreau hit the nail on the head when he said, "It is not enough to be industrious; so are the ants. What are you industrious about?"

How Far Are You Willing to Go?

The power of intention is the power to manifest, to create, to live a life of unlimited abundance, and to attract into your life the right people at the right moments.

—Wayne Dyer

If you want to move ahead, whether as an employee or an entrepreneur, you'll have to make major investments of time, resources, and effort. And through it all, expect to work, work, and work some more. Becoming a leader is hard work; but if being a leader is truly your destiny, if it's part of the brand you want to build, you'll find that you can do the work. You may be tired and you may wonder where it's all heading, but you'll be able to do what it takes to become the leader you were meant to be.

Many successful people were willing to sacrifice and take risks to get ahead. Yuli Ziv cashed out her retirement fund and put every dollar she had into building her Style Coalition.

Grant Cardone gave up his thrice-weekly golf game to focus on building what became a real estate empire worth $500 million.

Attorney Nafisé Nina Hodjat walked away from relationships with people she felt were too negative and might hinder her dream of creating what became the SLS Firm.

John Hanna moved into his mother's home while his wife moved into her sister's home so that they might save on rent and keep alive the dream of creating what became the Fairchild Group.

Tom Shieh and his wife moved into her parents' basement and put 90 percent of their income into building and growing their business, Crimcheck.

Other successful people have risked their reputations, suffered through bankruptcies, seen their marriages destroyed, risked their physical health working insane and punishing hours, surrendered control of their company to attract financing, swallowed their pride and asked for help, and done other unpleasant things so that they might succeed.

I'm not saying that suffering for the sake of suffering is a good idea. But you must ask yourself, what are you willing to set aside or to risk losing—at least for now—so that you can succeed?

Just how intentional are you? Are you willing to invest as much time, energy, financial resources, and whatever else it takes to achieve your dream?

There's nothing wrong with saying no, for not everyone is meant to be a whatever-it-takes type of entrepreneur or employee.

But if you do say yes, be prepared to work, live, and breathe intention.

Key Points

> *Work on Purpose, Play on Purpose, Rest on Purpose.*
> *Do not let yourself or anyone else waste your time.*
> —Izey Victoria Odiase

- Being intentional means knowing what we want and then focusing on the things that really matter. And what really matters are those things that take us closer to achieving our great dream.
- What are your actions saying about your degree of intentionality? Not your words but your actions.
- Intentionality is more than time. Being intentional also means being determined to improve, being aware of what you are doing at all times, pushing past your errors, tackling all sorts of unpleasant tasks, and asking for help—yet at the same time carving out time to protect your physical

and mental health and celebrating your small wins along the way.

- Never confuse being busy with being intentional. It's easy to find things to do—but is it necessary for you to do these things so that you might succeed? If not, you'll smother your intentions in make-work.

CHAPTER 6

Use Your Fear as Fuel

Everything you've ever wanted is on the other side of fear.

—George Adair

||||||||||||||||||||||||||||||||||||||||||||||||||||||

I had the honor of serving in the military for twenty years and found myself dodging mortar rounds more than once. From March 2004 through March 2005, I deployed for the second time in my military career to a new FOB (forward operating base) called Mulskinner—later named Camp Cuervo—in Iraq as the senior finance officer. There for not yet forty-eight hours, I received a call over my radio and heard a voice ask, "Terminator Six, do you copy?"

I replied that I did.

The person on the other end of the radio yelled, "Ma'am, we have incoming at eleven o'clock!" This meant that we were receiving enemy mortar rounds from the direction of the eleven on a clock dial. I recognized the voice on the radio. It was my detachment sergeant, waiting for me to give guidance on what everyone under my command should do to get out of the enemy line of fire—right now!

My boss was at a distant FOB, which meant I was the commander in charge of all finance personnel. It was at that moment that I realized I had to depend on my judgment, on what I thought to be the right way to respond to protect the lives of my soldiers. I held the radio for what seemed like an eternity, trying to devise the perfect plan based on scenarios I had learned in training. But the mortar rounds were getting closer, we were dispersed all over the FOB setting up our quarters, and a decision had to be made. My instincts kicked in; and I moved out, communicating over the radio, getting reports, and instructing soldiers on what to do. I no longer feared that saying or doing the wrong thing would make it seem like I didn't know what I was doing or that I was a failure. Lives depended on my ability to make decisions swiftly, so I moved decisively, operating on the 80 percent rule. That is, I am determined to move on with my plan now, even though it may not be the 100 percent solution for the situation.

In those few minutes, I learned that you don't have to give in to your fears and doubts. You can act and can make good decisions in a crisis even when, as I found, lives depend on it. Even if your brain is telling you that you don't have the right skillset, you can persevere as a leader.

Don't Let Fear Derail Your P²D

My fear of making the wrong decision in a dangerous situation caused me to hesitate. Fortunately, my fear of being seen as being indecisive fueled my drive to move out with a solution I hoped and prayed would keep everyone alive. For me at that time and in that situation, fear was both a stopper and a motivator. Unfortunately, for many people, fear is only a stopper, bringing their passion, perseverance, and drive to a crashing halt. Fear derails countless ambitious, inventive, creative people—even those burning with the desire to make something of themselves and make something big for their families.

Fear comes from countless sources and takes endless forms. For many of us, fear arises because we have internalized our childhoods and dread the consequences. We subconsciously feel that because we were raised in challenging, chaotic, abusive, neglectful, or other negative environments, we have no chance at success. We fear that we are doomed to stumble down the same path our parents did, so there is no reason to even try. When given a choice between two alternatives—such as starting a new business and remaining with the safe job we have—we often opt for the safer option, subconsciously feeling that this is "right" for us and is all we deserve. Others of us, even if we had happy childhoods, still fear failure for many reasons. But failure is our best mentor, so we should never fear it. And a surprising number of us fear success.

Sometimes our fears are well-founded, for we truly are unprepared to take on the new job or venture; we are not up to the challenge at the moment. Most of the time, however, our fears are fantasies, nightmares created by thoughts of a self-fulfilling prophecy.

The human brain is a powerful "protection machine" designed to keep us safe at all costs. This was vital when human existence was precarious when the wrong choice would leave us facing a hungry tiger, all alone and unarmed. Fear was our savior. To keep us safe, fear made us imagine that hungry tigers were lurking everywhere, that every loose rock presaged an avalanche, and that every stranger was a potential enemy.

Fear made us cling to the safety of the family or tribe, as well as to accustomed routines and ways of thought. This would keep us safe, we believed, and often that was true. But there was—and remains—a cost to this brain-generated, fear-safety equation. It meant that we always had to be cautious and wary of change. That we had to fit in perfectly with the family or tribe and with the accepted routines and ways of thought. That we could not deviate from the rules, norms, or customs; else, we be thrown out. And to be tossed out was to be at the mercy of tigers, avalanches, and enemies. To be on our own was dangerous and terrifying, so our protective brain urged us to do whatever it took to remain "in."

This is one of the reasons why, for example, many of us find it hard to imagine that we can rise above our unhappy past. Terrible though the past was, it was part and parcel of our family's norms and ways of thought and behavior. Being part of the family kept us alive, our brain tells us, and we cannot deviate from its rules and norms because deviation is dangerous. So we convince ourselves that we have no chance for a better life and should not even try. We are guided by a terrible fear, buried deep in the brain, that if we try to succeed, we will be pushed out. And to be out and alone is a terrifying prospect.

It is largely from this that our fear of failure, as well as our fear of success and many other fears, arises.

Fear works very hard to hold us back. But in many cases, the path we wish to journey takes us right up to our fear and it continues. Here is where we have the choice—and it's always our choice—to continue into our fear or to be derailed.

Using Fear to Move Ahead

*How we handle our fears will determine where we go
with the rest of our lives.*

—Judy Blume

|||||||||||||||||||||||||||||||||||||||||||||||||||||||

Our fears are very real and very powerful. We can't wish them away;
we can't ignore them. There is no medicine to "cure" them, no diet
or exercise routine that will cause them to melt away entirely. We
live with fear because fear is built into the human brain.

But while we live with fear, we do not have to surrender to it.
We can acknowledge it, examine it, test it, challenge it, and decide
what to do with it. We may sometimes accept and embrace the fear,
thankful that it is protecting us. And we may sometimes accept but
then set aside the fear, understanding that it is hindering us.

We can use our fear instead of being used by it. Rather than
running from fear, we can use it as a guide to show us what we need
to do. For a saleswoman, for example, fear of cold calling might
mean that she needs to work on separating rejection of a call from a
rejection of her, on understanding the harsh reality of cold-calling
statistics, and on whether this particular job is aligned with her
passion.

For an employee, fear of asking for a raise may mean that they
must work on building his skillset so that he genuinely is worthy
of more, developing relationships with potential mentors and new
bosses within the company, mastering techniques to calm anxiety,
and understanding his true value to the company and to the industry
at large.

For an entrepreneur, fear of signing that first big lease or taking
out that first big loan may mean that she has to strengthen her belief
in herself and her offering.

Rather than giving in, the saleswoman, employee, and

entrepreneur can embrace their fears as guides to greater success. They can calm their fears by doing the necessary work, building the necessary relationships, learning to envision the future in a positive way, and maintaining a growth mindset.

You can run from your fear or use it as an imaginary teacher sitting on your shoulder giving you new assignments. History is filled with people who faced their fears and succeeded beyond their wildest dreams. You can do the same. And yes, you will fail at various things along the way. Failure is a reality, just like fear. But just like fear, failure is a teacher. We can use our fears and failures as guides to success. I have learned that my latest failure oftentimes is my greatest teacher.

What Do We Fear?

*If you can't fly, then run. If you can't run, then walk.
If you can't walk then crawl, but whatever you do, you
have to keep moving forward.*

—Martin Luther King Jr.

||||||||||||||||||||||||||||||||||||||||||||||||||||

There are many well-known common fears, such as fear of darkness, heights, closed spaces, snakes, germs, flying, and more. Then there are fears more specific to employees and entrepreneurs. Among other things, employees may fear:

- **Feeling not being good enough**—even if they have the required job skills and certifications, plus the official schooling and on-the-job experience, many employees feel as if they're not up to the job. They're not confident in their abilities or their value, they internalize a lack of constant accolades as a signal that they are failures, they feel they fall short compared to their peers, they suffer from impostor syndrome, they focus on their past errors, and they otherwise demote themselves in their minds.

- **Being publicly criticized by the boss**—just the thought of being dressed down in front of others can be mortifying. Even if you agree that you made a mistake, being publicly chastised may make you feel that you're not good enough. And if you feel that you haven't made a mistake, you may believe that you're being treated unfairly.

- **Being embarrassed in front of others**—many are afraid that if they ask questions, they'll show their fellow employees how inadequate they are; and if they make a mistake, they'll be branded unintelligent and shunned.

- **Being demoted or fired**—the threat of losing some or all your paycheck and of having your career derailed or destroyed is rightfully terrifying to many.

  Entrepreneurs share many of the same fears as employees, including not being good enough and being embarrassed in front of others. In addition, they may fear:

- **Not being up to the job**—being an entrepreneur means you'll have to make major decisions in many areas where you have no training or experience. Think of a scientifically minded engineer who has invented a wildly successful app and now finds himself responsible for okaying the company logo and PR campaign, deciding which candidate for chief human resources officer to hire, and poring over thick stacks of detailed financials. It's the rare inventor-entrepreneur who feels comfortable with all these tasks.

- **Being buffeted by larger forces**—the entrepreneur may be the boss; but she and her company will be buffeted by changes in the economy, changes in taste and society, and other factors completely beyond her control. As an employee, she can leave dealing with these problems to others. But as the boss, it's all on her shoulders.

- **Being rejected**—the entrepreneur's venture isn't just "some company" they happen to be helming. They came up with the original idea, they birthed and nourished the company, and their identity and feelings of self-worth are wrapped all around the company. Yet from the moment they began turning their idea into reality, they have faced rejection. Rejection from investors and banks who refuse to give them money, from suppliers who aren't interested in the business, from talented people who decline offers of employment, from customers who turn their noses up at offerings, and more. A thousand rejections are baked into the creation, growth, and maintenance of a company; and the entrepreneur may feel each and every one as a personal rebuff.

- **Failing**—a lot can ride on the entrepreneur's success, including the livelihoods of dozens or hundreds of employees counting on her or him to make this all work. "If I fail," the entrepreneur realizes, "I will have cut off all their paychecks."

We often respond to fear by turning away. We delay dealing with issues that trigger our fear, and we suddenly find dozens of other things that demand our immediate attention. We decide to throw ourselves into some completely unrelated project; or we just sit in the office, staring at the computer all day long, getting nothing done.

We can conjure up endless fears and "fix" them in countless ways that only hold us back.

Action, the Antidote to Fear

You don't need to see the whole staircase. Just take the first step.

—Martin Luther King Jr.

||||||||||||||||||||||||||||||||||||||||||||||||||||||||

Many of us rationalize when slowed down or paralyzed by our fears. We tell ourselves that it is wise to hold back because we're not prepared. Taking any kind of action would be dangerous, we assure ourselves, because we lack so many things at the moment. We lack knowledge, skills, contacts, contracts, financing, marketing savvy, certifications, and so much more. We tell ourselves that our fears are smart, for they will keep us out of danger. We praise ourselves for being so careful, for refusing to leap without looking, and for spending even more time devising our plans. We will happily spend forever perfecting our plans, but when we are ruled by fear, no plan is perfect enough.

Fear freezes action. We may seem to be very busy when we are fearful, but our fear prevents us from being active where and how it matters. Fear equals inaction, and the best response to fear is targeted action.

Your first targeted action should be to acknowledge that fear is absolutely normal. It's built into our brains, and there's nothing we can do about this evolutionary fact.

The next targeted action should be to understand that failure is inevitable. Everybody fails—even huge successes like Bill Gates, whose first computer company flopped. He later committed what some consider to be the worst business error ever when he rescued Apple from dissolving, only to see it overtake Microsoft in many ways. He also totally misread the importance of the Internet and allowed Google to soundly thrash Microsoft's Bing search engine. Another fiasco, which Gates says is his "greatest mistake ever," was failing to create an operating system for smartphones, which allowed Google to dominate the market with its Android system.[12] The dollar cost of these failures amounts to billions!

So acknowledge the fact that you will fail now and then. Then embrace the fact that by showing you what doesn't work, failure brings you closer to discovering what will. Thomas Watson Sr., the driving force behind IBM's rise to dominance in the middle part of the twentieth century, knew that mistakes can be marvelous teachers. At one point, an employee made a mistake that cost the company $600,000, which was quite a bit of money back then. But Watson did not fire the man. Instead, Watson pointed out that he had just spent over half a million dollars training the man, and he wouldn't make that mistake again.

So when you feel fear settling in, don't back off and don't stop. Instead, act. Pick something you can do and pick it now. Give yourself a reasonable amount of time to do it—and then do it! Don't worry if it's the perfect action for the moment, and don't worry whether you are perfectly prepared to do it. Just do it.

Don't bury yourself in crafting the ideal action plan; instead, remind yourself that spending all that time creating the perfect plan is doomed to failure because conditions change, often rapidly so. During the months or years you spend trying to create the perfect plan, the economy may change, your industry will change, and your competitors will launch plans of their own. The people you're relying on for assistance will start looking for other projects or opportunities when they realize that your planning may drag on forever, and any marketing and advertising you've been doing will go stale. Plus, your customers or clients aren't going to wait forever.

PepsiCo CEO Indra Nooyi has warned about attaching yourself

---

[12] Mary Hanbury, "Bill Gates says his 'greatest mistake ever' was failing to create Android at Microsoft," BusinessInsider.com (June 24, 2019), accessed January 12, 2022, https://www.businessinsider.com/bill-gates-greatest-mistake-not-creating-android-microsoft-2019-6.

---

to a fixed plan. She points out that "if you always have one eye on some future goal, you stop paying attention to the job at hand, miss opportunities that might arise, and stay fixedly on one path, even when a better, newer course might have opened up."[13]

Another problem with over-planning is that it allows you to indulge your fears. You tell yourself that you don't have to deal with your fears because "the plan" will solve all your problems. But fears don't magically vanish. You learn how to deal with your fears by facing them head on. Yes, it's important to plan, but planning only takes you so far—you need *action* to cover the full distance. Don't wait until you've created the 100 percent perfect plan because even a perfect plan is worthless if it's executed too late. Shoot for the 80 percent solution, and you'll find that the mere fact that you're taking action will invigorate you and help quell any fears.

So pick the thing that you can do now or has the largest impact or carries you forward to the next item. If you can't figure out what that is, then just pick one thing to do—now. Even if it's not the best or most impactful thing, the fact that you can and will do it makes it the best and most impactful action for now. It takes you one step forward. It takes one item off the to-do list. It takes away a source of stress. It helps clarify the confusion. And it gives you a bit of success—something you can build on.

Fear of not having the right business background was a major hindrance for me as I set out to create IFAS. My business plan was complete; but I hesitated, thinking I was not ready to be the successful businessperson that I had seen, read about, and admired on TV and in magazines.

My short-term goal, carefully spelled out in my plan, was to open a CPA firm providing tax and QuickBooks services to small

---

[13] E. Napoletano, "Notable Quotables: Inspiring Words From History's Women Business Leaders." AmericanExpress.com. accessed January 30, 2022, https://www.americanexpress.com/en-us/business/trends-and-insights/articles/notable-quotables-inspiring-words-historys-female-business-leaders/.

companies. To carry this plan through, I had to become a CPA. Passing the necessary exam might have been easy because my undergraduate degree was in accounting. But all my experience was in accounting for appropriated and non-appropriated federal government dollars, which had somewhat different methodologies than accounting in the civilian world. I studied for the CPA exam by attending a CPA review course and took two parts of the CPA exam but did not pass. I was three months into my business, had only done three tax returns, had one QuickBooks client with a $200 budget, and was still not a CPA. My big dream of building a multimillion-dollar business was fading rapidly. I knew something had to change—but what?

According to my business plan, starting a CPA practice was my short-term goal while moving on to government contracting—accounting for federal-appropriated and non-appropriated dollars—was my long-term goal. But government contracting seemed like a convoluted maze of confusion. It frightened me, so I put it on the back burner while pursuing what I thought would be the easy route.

I started my company in January, and in March of the same year, I attended a government contracting workshop given by the U.S. Army Small Business Program Office. During the presentation, the government spoke about its goal of doing more business with minorities, women, and service-disabled veterans. They explained how to go about working with the government and the types of products and services that they bought. As I sat there listening, I couldn't believe my ears: my capabilities and the experience I had gained through my military career were services that the federal government was buying. Not only that, I was a woman, a minority, and a service-disabled veteran!

The lightbulb went off in my head, and immediately, my long-term business goal became my immediate goal. Right then and there, I began marketing myself as a federal financial management accounting firm, promoting myself to the other attendees at my table.

My fear of leaping into this industry vanished, and my confidence grew tremendously just from knowing what I had heard. I went with what I knew, and my natural instincts kicked in. I had been battle-tested and honed to think quickly on my feet, and now I was pulling from experience to secure my new position. I did not want to miss out on the opportunity to network with potential partners and customers. Even though my printed material talked about taxes and QuickBooks, I was determined to market myself as a service-disabled female veteran who owned a federal financial management accounting firm.

It must have worked because a few months later, I got a call from a business owner, one of the people sitting at my table at that seminar. She was looking for a partner on a contract with the army. It seems that one of her key employees was out and wasn't sure if she was returning. That vacant slot needed to be filled immediately. My "table contact" asked if my company could serve as a subcontractor, filling in the vacant slot with someone very similar to the person who had left. Since my company consisted of just me, I had no one to offer. I was a consulting company, not a staffing company. But when I hung up the phone, I realized that I had the background needed to fill the position. So I looked in the mirror and said to myself, *You're hired!* In other words, I filled the job with me!

A week later, I was serving as both the employer and the employee on my very first subcontract—this after being in business for four months as a government contractor and seven months total. I eventually hired someone to replace me and grew the subcontract substantially over the ten years it was in place. Not only did this subcontract reduce my fear of operating in the market, but it also increased my confidence as a business owner.

Steps to Ameliorating the Fear

Our fears do not magically disappear when we've taken an action or reached a certain point. They do not vanish once we sign that first lease or hire the tenth employee or get the perfect client. We do not suddenly become cool and confident just because we have been promoted, developed the ideal logo, or made a great pitch to the board.

We constantly face new situations, new challenges, and new fears. Or perhaps they're the same old fears in new guises. While we cannot banish fear, we can learn to think about it in new ways. Suppose you fear that you are an impostor—that someone will soon realize that you don't have the proper experience, degrees, certificates, background, or whatever. Is your impostor fear pushing you to chase after degrees, certifications, and awards to prove to yourself that you are the real thing? And are you overworking and burning out, trying to prove you are not an impostor? If so, stop, step back, and look around. Most likely, you'll see that you have all the requirements for the job or nearly enough of them. Rather than trying to double the size of your résumé, ask yourself if you're really using all the knowledge and skills that you already have. Ask yourself if you're using your existing network, working closely with your mentors, and inspiring your peers to create the best possible working environment in which you can flourish.

Suppose you fear that you will fail. What can you do when that sickening feeling of impending doom hits your stomach? You can plot things out. Think through what will happen if you totally flop. Maybe you'll lose your job, you'll have to move in with your parents, you'll be humiliated, and more. Put yourself in a place of total failure and then ask yourself: Am I still alive? Do I still have my brain? Do I still have my passion, perseverance, and drive? If so, nothing else matters.

I know of one man, Bill Dore, who made exactly such a "what if

I fail" list. He was about to risk everything he had to buy a struggling company called Global Divers that supplied underwater divers to oil companies—divers who repaired oil rigs off the southern coast of the United States. He wrote the list and decided that even if he lost all his money plus his house and his reputation in the industry, he would still have the teaching credential he had earned several years before. He could always support his family by being a high school sports coach. He took the risk and turned a company facing bankruptcy into a global giant.

And by the way, if you do fail, you'll be in good company because even huge successes have belly-flopped. Martha Stewart went from being world-famous for her homemaking tips, products, and *Martha Stewart Living* magazine to being incarcerated. Yet she bounced back and is now worth hundreds of millions of dollars. Bill Bartmann, whose Commercial Financial Services (CFS) debt-collection company made him one of the richest men in America, saw it all come crashing down. He was forced into bankruptcy; but he built back, and his new company, CFS2, earned $10 million in a single year.[14]

Suppose you fear that no one will back your new idea. That you're not good enough. That the competition will thrash you. For every fear your brain can thrust at you, there is a way to think through it and see it in a different light. The same brain that created a fear can find a way around it if you give it a chance.

---

[14] Deep Patel, "9 Multimillionaires Who Lost It All but Came Back," *Entrepreneur* (June 17, 2019), Accessed January 12, 2022. https://www.entrepreneur.com/article/335042.

Give Yourself a Chance

It is your choices and decisions that determine your destiny.

—Roy T. Bennett

|||||||||||||||||||||||||||||||||||||||||||||||||||||||

Action is the antidote to fear, and there's a powerful action you can take now when you're not in the grip of fright.

Ask yourself a question: What scares me? Is it cold calling? Asking for a raise? Standing up to a nasty coworker? Something else? Make a list of those fears that you recognize. Now ask yourself: what fears do I not recognize? The answer won't be obvious because, by definition, these are the fears you do not acknowledge. So ask yourself: What tasks cause me to slow down, dive into distractions, or spin endless plans that never seem perfect enough? What tasks extinguish the flame of my P^{2}D? These are the fears you have not admitted to.

Then ask yourself: What fears am I using as a crutch? That is, which fears have you turned into "positives"? Have you convinced yourself that you cannot even think about opening your business until you get two more degrees and three more certificates? That asking for a raise may get you fired, so you should be absolutely satisfied with what you have? That you'll never get financing, so there's no point in filling out all those lengthy applications?

Finally, ask yourself what you are way too comfortable doing and whether you are doing that comfortable thing over and over as an excuse to hide from your fears. In other words, how much time are you spending in your comfort zone versus out of it?

Now you know which fears you recognize, which you aren't acknowledging, and which you are using as a crutch. Just knowing what holds you back is a great start! Now remind yourself that almost none of these fears are protecting you. Yes, a few fears are relevant.

It's probably good to fear asking the boss for a raise the first week on the job or sign a lease for a suite of pricey offices before you've signed your first client. But most fears are just thoughts produced by an overly protective brain. They tell us that danger is everywhere. They prevent us from learning, exploring, and growing.

But that's exactly what we need to do when we're fearful: learn, explore, and grow.

We need to learn, for example, about the specifics of the thing we fear. We may need to learn that while 90 percent or more of cold calls end in no, the small number of times we hear maybe or "Let's talk some more" or yes is all it takes to make us a sales superstar! We also need to learn about the specifics of our potential customers, what they need, and how they like to be approached.

We need to grow both professionally and personally. We need to find teachers and mentors to guide us. We need to learn about successful salespeople to inspire us. We need to learn how to separate a "cold-call no" from personal rejection. We need to learn how to settle down properly after a difficult day of calling, avoiding harmful habits that set us up for disaster in the long run.

And we need to learn how to keep our eyes and hopes fixed in the future. But not any future and certainly not the future painted by the fearful brain. Instead, we can visualize success. We can ask ourselves: What's on the other side of this fear? What's behind the wall, across the river, through the next door? What can we accomplish when we use fear as a stepping stone to success?

Once we've learned, explored, and shifted focus to the possibilities, it's time to take action. Better yet, take action now while we are still in the process of learning, exploring, and growing. The small action we take now will move us a little closer to the goal and give us the confidence to throw ourselves into learning, exploring, and growing.

Mental resilience and discipline are key attributes needed to build the staying power it takes to persevere. So make taking action your duty, your obligation, and your promise to yourself. And then do what you need to do!

Always remember, there is never a perfect time to start a business, sell a business, or move to the next step in your career. Don't wait for the perfect time that will never be. Act and perfect your actions as you advance.

Don't Hold Back

If fear is holding you back, remind yourself that you are very good at what you do. You've prepared yourself, and you've mastered the knowledge or skills. You can perform at a very high level. And if you miss the mark or make a mistake, congratulations! Every successful person and everyone who has mastered their destiny has made plenty of mistakes, some of the whoppers. Now that you've made a mistake, now that you've humiliated yourself or tossed away lots of money, you're just like them.

Don't let fear hold you back. Don't be disabled by fear of being embarrassed or by fear of being seen as a failure. And don't be held back by the fear that you are doomed to failure because of where you started in life or because of your poor family with addiction and abuse issues. You can rise above, and you can break generational curses. You do not have to be who your parents and grandparents were. You can be the person you want and deserve to be.

Key Points

- Fear is often the "break in the tracks" that derails our progress. Sometimes our fears are well-grounded, but most of the time, they are fantasies created by a brain run wild.
- While fear is a genuine emotion, we need not surrender to it. We can use fear as a guide just as we can use failure as a teacher.

- The antidote to fear is action. When fear threatens to paralyze us, the best response is to act and take an action that moves us further ahead.
- Thought is also an antidote to fear, for if you think your fears through to their ultimate end, you usually find that they are not scary after all.
- All successful people have failed at one point. But they pushed past fear by learning, exploring, and growing. Learning, exploring, and growing, combined with taking action, are the keys to turning fear into success.

CHAPTER 7

Find Your Higher Purpose

The purpose of life is a life of purpose.
—Robert Byrne

|||||||||||||||||||||||||||||||||||||||||||||||||||||

Oprah Winfrey was born to an unmarried teenager who worked as a housemaid. She lived with her grandmother for the first six years of her life. She was so poor that she often wore dresses her grandmother had made out of potato sacks, which provoked a great deal of laughter and mockery from other children. Oprah suffered sexual abuse at the hand of relatives and a family friend became pregnant at age fourteen and saw her baby die shortly after birth.

That's just a brief description of the well-known tragic life experience she suffered. Even better known is her phenomenal success as a talk show host, actress, producer, and more. Over the course of her storied career, she accumulated many honors and quite a bit of money, heading the Forbes 2009 list of Wealthiest Black Americans.[15] And she was the only billionaire on the list.

Oprah is also one of the most generous Americans, having donated hundreds of millions of dollars to education and other causes. She donated $10 million to help victims of Hurricane Katrina and created the Oprah Winfrey Leadership Academy for Girls in South Africa. The academy project was close to her heart;

---

[15] Matthew Miller, "The Wealthiest Black Americans," *Forbes* (May 6, 2009), accessed April 13, 2022, https://www.forbes.com/2009/05/06/richest-black-americans-busienss-billionaires-richest-black-americans.html?sh=3ef66aca956e.

she wanted to help girls who, like her, grew up with little money and opportunity but were given financial support in their quest to become educated and rise above their circumstances.

Defining Higher Purpose

Oprah had a powerful higher purpose, driven by her early-life experiences. She found great meaning in giving to help others just as others had given to help her.

Some people distinguish between "higher purpose" and "meaning in life." I prefer to think of them as being one and the same: something (or things) that infuses life with joy and satisfaction specifically because it lifts us up out of ourselves and connects us with others. Having purpose or meaning fills us with the feeling that we are doing more, much more, than simply going through the motions called life. Instead, we are making a positive impact on the world in one way or another.

Higher purpose in life often involves directly helping others, but it doesn't have to. For many people, there is great meaning in singing in choirs or participating in other activities that bring people together for shared joy or shared work. Of course, we tend to hear more about those whose purpose and meaning involve giving money. Robert F. Smith demonstrated tremendous purpose when, while delivering a speech to the 2019 graduating class of Morehouse College, he announced that he would pay off all their student loans. Just shy of four hundred students were in that graduating class, and the cost to the generous billionaire was somewhere near $10 million.[16] Smith is not alone in expressing his higher purpose by

---

[16] Allison Klein, "Billionaire Robert F. Smith pledges to pay off Morehouse College Class of 2019's student loans." *The Washington Post* (May 19, 2019), accessed February 10, 2022. https://www.washingtonpost.com/lifestyle/2019/05/19/billionaire-robert-f-smith-pledges-pay-off-morehouse-college-class-s-student-loans/.

giving money. Warren Buffett has given $42.8 billion to improve health and alleviate poverty. Bill and Melinda Gates have given $29.8 billion for similar causes. MacKenzie Scott has given $5.83 billion to racial, gender, and economic inequality causes. Mark Zuckerberg and his wife, Priscilla Chan, have given nearly $3 billion to support science, education, and other causes.[17] Charles "Chuck" Feeney, the former owner of the Oakland A's baseball team, gave $8 billion to support science and human rights.

A higher purpose doesn't have to involve donating money. Jimmy Carter's actions as president of the United States did not propel him to the top of any leadership lists. Yet he is considered one of the most admired men living today—and for good reason. Since leaving the Oval Office, he has devoted himself to bettering the world by helping to negotiate peaceful ends to global conflicts, working to improve human rights, eradicating devastating diseases, and building homes for the needy—literally building, with a hammer in his now-very-old hands.

Many millions of people also find meaning in helping others. You may have never heard of Elizabeth "Betty" Podgurski, but she has been honored for her more than ten thousand hours of volunteer work at Brigham and Women's Faulkner Hospital. "I just like helping people," she explained.[18]

---

[17] Angel Au-Yeung, Deniz Cam, Kerry A. Dolan, et al., "The 25 Most Philanthropic Billionaires," *Forbes* (January 19, 2021), accessed February 10, 2022https://www.forbes.com/sites/forbeswealthteam/2021/01/19/americas-top-givers-the-25-most-philanthropic-billionaires/?sh=595ac6761f59.

[18] Brigham and Women's Faulkner Hospital, "Dedicated volunteer honored for 10,000 plus hours of service" (Undated), accessed February 12, 2022, https://www.brighamandwomensfaulkner.org/about-bwfh/news/dedicated-volunteer-honored-for-10000-plus-hours-of-service.

Higher Purpose Gives Strength

The best way to lengthen out our days is to walk steadily and with a purpose.

—Charles Dickens

For some, striving to find a higher purpose is natural. Perhaps the desire is born into us, or we learn how gratifying it can be to look beyond our desires as we grow up. Or maybe the yearning for a higher purpose develops later in life when we're financially settled and can turn our thoughts to meaning in life. For still other people, a higher purpose develops out of a life experience, such as the loss of a child.

But while many people naturally come upon their higher purpose, others need to put some thought into finding it. And some people wonder if they should bother thinking about purpose now when they're struggling so hard to lead or to build a business or climb the corporate ladder.

I believe that it's always valuable to have a higher purpose. I believe we must have one, for we were put on this earth to work hard, earn money, and pay it forward by sharing it with others and doing good things for the world. Identifying our higher purpose helps us align our actions with our moral obligation.

Being a leader, working to create a new company, and climbing the corporate ladder are serious and often strenuous endeavors. Having a higher purpose helps us keep pushing ahead when the inevitable obstacles arise. That's because having a purpose energizes us, lights up our P^2D, and helps us push ahead no matter what tries to slow us down. Knowing that we have to succeed so that we may buy our mother a house or build a gym at our old school for the next generation of students keeps us focused and energized.

And having a higher purpose can make us healthier. Research

shows that adults who felt their lives were meaningful felt physically and mentally healthier compared to those who were still searching for meaning.[19]

Imagine that you find yourself in a position like Jeff Immelt did just a few days after becoming CEO of General Electric. He had barely settled into his office when, on 9/11, three hijacked airliners were deliberately crashed into the World Trade Center and the Pentagon, and a fourth one crashed in a Pennsylvania field. GE owned GE Aviation, which leased airplanes, and air travel was about to take a big hit. GE also had major interests in insurance. In fact, they had issued reinsurance on the World Trade Center, which meant they could be on the hook for huge sums of money. GE owned NBC, and advertising was down following 9/11. In fact, for three days following 9/11, NBC broadcast without commercials, which forced GE to take a billion-dollar write-off. Day after day, Immelt was forced to make major decisions on issues in the sprawling company he had just taken control of, and he was often not fully up to speed on the issues. Then, when things seemed to be getting under control, a package containing anthrax powder was sent to NBC at *30 Rock*, and they had to close down the entire building. If you were sitting in Immelt's chair at that moment, wouldn't you like to be in the best physical and mental shape possible?

Immelt has said that in times of crises like these, "You learn to hold two truths. You learn to say, 'Things can always get worse, but

---

[19] See, for example, 1) Sanja Gupta, "Purpose in Life Is Good for Your Health." *Everyday Health*, reviewed December 7, 2015, accessed February 12, 2022, https://www.everydayhealth.com/news/purpose-life-good-your-health/. 2) "Finding meaning in life could improve your health" (Harvard Health Publishing: April 1, 2020), accessed February 12, 2022, https://www.health.harvard.edu/mind-and-mood/finding-meaning-in-life-could-improve-your-health#:~:text=Respondents%20who%20believed%20they%20had,with%20those%20who%20didn't.&text=More%20meaning%20in%20one's%20life,less%20stressed%2C%20suggest%20the%20researchers. Accessed February 12, 2022.

here's a dream that I have for the future, and I'm not going to give up on that.'"[20]

Not only can having a purpose or meaning in life make us physically and mentally stronger, but it can also clarify what we are trying to achieve and why it is so important to stick to the goal even in the face of incredible difficulty.

Luckily, most of us will never find ourselves in such a terrible position as Immelt did. But we may find ourselves facing problems and disasters, financial crises, and loss of support. We may be pressured to back down or resign, accept conditions we would not normally tolerate, and otherwise be pushed to the wall.

This is inevitable. What's not inevitable is how we respond and whether we have the purpose and meaning that give us the physical strength, emotional health, and mental clarity that allow us to triumph over adversity.

---

[20] Polina Pompliano, "Ex-GE CEO Jeff Immelt on Leading Through Crisis, Taking Personal Responsibility, and Becoming a Master of Chaos," *The Profile* (May 18, 2021), accessed February 12, 2022, https://theprofile.substack. com/p/ex-ge-ceo-jeff-immelt-on-leading.

Higher Purpose Equals Better Business

Having a higher purpose is more than just about profits. You actually end up making more profits in the long run because employees really are a lot more engaged and customers see the higher purpose in the company.

—Tony Hsieh

|||||||||||||||||||||||||||||||||||||||||||||||||||||||||

Not only is having a higher purpose good for you personally, but it's also good for your business. Employees who believe in your purpose, who feel they are doing something meaningful, are better workers because they care about what they are doing. Their commitment and enthusiasm are transmitted to customers, who are more likely to want to have an ongoing relationship with your company. Even if customers don't know what your company's purpose is, they can sense the vibes coming from purpose-driven employees—as opposed to a company whose workers are just going through the motions to hit minimal goals. And according to a LinkedIn survey, "71% of professionals say they would be willing to take a pay cut to work for a company that has a mission they believe in and shared values."[21]

You can often see the leader's purpose in the way the company approaches its employees and customers. Bansi Lakhani, founder and chair of Healing Hands, imbued her company with a higher purpose by changing a key business question from "How much of

---

[21] Nina McQueen, "Workplace Culture Trends: The Key to Hiring (and Keeping) Top Talent in 1028," LinkedIn Official Blog (June 26, 2018), accessed February 13, 2022, https://blog.linkedin.com/2018/june/26/workplace-culture-trends-the-key-to-hiring-and-keeping-top-talent."

this can we sell?" to "How can this product help my customers?"[22] The outdoor-adventure chain REI encourages its employees to adopt its goals of protecting the earth by becoming carbon-neutral, embracing the circular economy, and advancing racial equality. The company aims to "put purpose before profits and act in the long-term interests of our members and community."[23]

None of these goals are necessarily better than the others. It doesn't matter if the leader's higher purpose concerns the employees, customers, or the community. The point is that when the leader's higher purpose reaches into every corner of the business, that organization attracts employees who embrace, or come to embrace, that same purpose. And that is good for business.

Zappos, the online shoe company, went to extremes to ensure its employees embraced its purpose. Every new hire went through a training program in which they learned about the company's values. When they finished training, each new employee was offered money to *not work* at Zappos. The company was saying, "If you don't embrace our culture, for whatever reason, we're not a good match. And we're so passionate about finding employees who love our purpose that if you don't love it, we'll pay you to go elsewhere."

---

[22] Marcel Schwantes, "5 Leaders Share Their No. 1 Tip for Building (and Sustaining) a Purpose-Drive Business." *Inc.* (undated), accessed February 12, 2022, https://www.inc.com/marcel-schwantes/how-to-build-purpose-driven-business.html.

[23] 2020 Impact Report. REI (undated), accessed February 12, 2022, https://www.rei.com/stewardship.

Finding Higher Purpose

The two most important days in life are the day you are
born and the day you discover the reason why.
—Mark Twain

||||||||||||||||||||||||||||||||||||||||||||||||||||||||||

Some people never have to think about what their higher purpose may be. They have known what it is before they were even aware of the concept. Others struggle to find our purpose. And it's no wonder, for life is full of demands, distractions, deadlines, and decisions we must wrestle with. We're often buried deep in work and family responsibilities, and when we have a free moment, we just want to forget about everything and relax.

But it need not take long to discover your higher purpose or, at least, figure out a few potential purposes. Nothing says you have to find your purpose in a single aha moment. It may take several tries to find what brings meaning to your life. Or your purpose may evolve over time as you change.

As you begin your quest to find your higher purpose, think about what makes you feel alive and useful. What makes you feel as if you're doing more than going through the motions every day?

One approach to answering that question is to engage in "giving activities," things that have you helping others. It doesn't have to be formal and time-consuming; you can simply be friendly and helpful to the other people at work and to those you encounter as you go about your daily business. Greet them cheerfully. If it's appropriate, greet them by name and ask how their day is going. If they need a hand, offer to help. You can also take a more formal approach, joining in charitable or social activities such as volunteering at a hospital, cleaning up the neighborhood park, or delivering food to people unable to shop on their own.

You may find meaning in your experiences. I know that I did.

I didn't grow up in a neighborhood rife with opportunities or filled with examples of people like me who succeeded in building million-dollar businesses. But as a youth, I was in Junior Achievement; and every so often, business owners would come and speak to us. It was very exciting to see them come in all dressed up and carrying briefcases and to learn about the kind of businesses they had. I just didn't see this in my neighborhood. Their achievements helped me dream bigger than I would have, and their generosity stuck with me.

So several years back, I started the NextGen Leadership Academy. It is a two-week mini-MBA program in which we teach high school students, often from disadvantaged areas, about entrepreneurship and business plan creation. We take them from the beginning of the process to the end. The students come up with some pretty amazing ideas and do the financials and marketing pieces for their proposals. We have business people come in to talk to them about their experience in business. My oldest son, who is also an entrepreneur and serves as executive director for the Arches to Better Economic Empowerment (TABEE), the nonprofit that I started—serves as the lead instructor at the high school that I graduated from for the NextGen Program.

We put the kids from Jennings Senior High School in St. Louis into different groups; and each has to come up with a business plan, which they present to the business people, and the best plan wins. Then I take the kids in the winning group to Washington DC, where IFAS is based. One time, I took the winning group to see, among other things, a sports complex called The St. James. They have an indoor golf simulator, a track, batting cages, and a gym; and it is owned by two African American men. One of the men took us through the complex, listened to the group's pitch, and gave them feedback on their business plan. The kids were just blown away that this black man owned all this because where they come from, and where I came from, you just don't see that.

Of course, we did more than visit The St. James on this trip.

Throughout their stay, the kids had a driver and were required to dress up in suits and dresses. Hopefully, I left them with the same uplifting impression that Junior Achievement left with me. It will be even more rewarding if they pay it forward once they get to where they're going.

Looking into your life story may give you ideas for discovering your higher purpose. For example:

- Have you suffered a wrong that you would like to correct? Or would you like to assist others who have suffered the same wrong?
- Have you been helped by others? Perhaps a teacher, good friend, charity, or local church group gave you an assist?
- Has something bothered you since you were young? Were you upset seeing homeless people living on the streets or learning in school about environmental problems or social inequities?
- Do you absolutely love your city, state, or country and want to make it a better place for everyone?
- Did you grow up in a troubled family or environment and found solace or inspiration in a certain place or activity? Perhaps the youth center or your school's drama club?
- Was there someone you really admired when you were growing up? Perhaps a civic leader, teacher, doctor, relative, or family friend? Someone whom you thought was doing something important, interesting, or special?
- Did you know people who seemed especially content with their lives?
- Did you know people whom others praised a lot?
- Did people comment on some special quality in you? Perhaps your kindness or eagerness to learn? Maybe a certain talent you had or your willingness to protect other kids from bullies?

Asking yourself these and other questions may uncover your purpose in life. You may also wish to explore your higher purpose through religion, whether on your own or through an established church or other organization.

Another approach to finding your higher purpose is to think about what's lacking in your workplace, family, community, ethnic or religious group, and other circles. In your family, it may be a lack of connection. In your workplace, it may be a lack of opportunities for recognition and upward mobility. In your community, it may be a lack of social services or open spaces. In your ethnic or religious group, it may be a lack of acceptance. These various lacks may not have affected you personally, but you may discover a great deal of meaning in helping others deal with the problem(s).

Yet another idea is to seek out and surround yourself with people who have already found their higher purposes. Being around them and seeing what they do and talk about may give you ideas for finding your purpose. You might also think about what you enjoy doing and then see if you can share it with others. If you love carving wood, for example, you might find purpose in carving beautiful objects and donating them. If you love singing, you might join a choir and find purpose in sharing beautiful music with others. Or volunteering to entertain at senior centers or teaching music to children.

There are many other approaches to finding your higher purpose. The key thing to remember is that you're looking for the cause that you feel you were born to do, something that fills you with hope and confidence and motivates you to such an extent that you are willing to face all obstacles. It may be as big as creating a huge foundation. Or it may be much simpler, as in training guide dogs to be given to people you've never met. It doesn't matter what form your higher purpose takes as long as it fills your life with meaning.

As you seek your purpose, remember that it's not exactly the same thing as happiness. Finding your purpose will bring joy and happiness to your life, but the happiness that comes from indulging yourself does not bring purpose to your life. Eating a big slab of cake or winning the lottery may make you happy for the moment but won't fill your life with purpose. On the other hand, sharing your cake with others or donating part of your lottery winnings to the needy may point you to your purpose. And don't confuse checking items off your to-do list with meaning in life. Yes, meeting goals can be satisfying and make you more organized at work and play, but living a busy life is not the same thing as living a meaningful life.

A Note to Employees

It can be difficult for employees to find purpose in their work, especially at lower levels. When you're standing by a cash register all day, ringing up one customer after another, or stuffing items into boxes on an assembly line, your work can seem somewhat meaningless. This may not be a problem if you find meaning in other activities and just go to work for the paycheck. But if you intend to move up the ladder to become a leader, you'll have to find a higher purpose tied to your work.

If your employer does not have a community outreach program linked to your purpose, see if your company will support your purpose. Many companies allow employees to take time off for worthy causes, and some will even match your donations to a cause.

Here at IFAS, we have a Corporate Citizenship Board made up of employees. They review donation requests coming in from employees everywhere in the organization and decide which ones to support. One year, an employee who had an autistic child asked the board if IFAS would participate in a walk for autism. The Corporate Citizenship Board looked at the request and recommended that we support it. So we donated funds, and a group of us participated in the walk on behalf of the employee's child.

We also have an annual day of giving. One year, we supported the homeless, and IFAS employees in five or six states went out and supported homeless shelters by donating items and serving food. The entire company participated.

Another time, we decided to help the kids from a disadvantaged elementary school that didn't have Internet connectivity. We funded laptops for an entire class of fifth graders and went and watched them unpack and set up their computers. The kids were so excited and appreciative, and their parents were there as well. The children used their computers throughout the school year and at the end of the year visited the IFAS headquarters location, where they presented their "thank-you presentation" in our conference room. They were all dressed up, with ties for the boys and dresses for the girls. They told us how they had used their laptops and what a difference it had made in their lives. I'll always remember one girl who said, "Now, on a snow day, I can get on my computer and do work!" This was years before the COVID-19 pandemic, so working remotely during a snow day was exciting for those children.

Giving back and staying connected to the communities that we live and work in always has been a part of our mission at IFAS. And our employees really love being able to give back. I didn't realize how much they would embrace that—but they really, really enjoy giving back.

If your employer won't support your personal higher purposes, and you don't resonate with any purpose the company has, you might still find purpose on the job by helping others at work. You might also focus on your customers or clients and find meaning in helping them solve problems. If you have a lot of experience or special skills, you might find purpose in training or mentoring others. If you're learning a lot on the job, you might view this job as a stepping stone to something better and find meaning in that.

You might also find purpose by understanding the larger picture. Let's say that you spend the workday punching out ugly little metal plates and have no idea what happens to them once they leave your work area. You're bored and don't really care if you do a good job or not. You only work hard enough to keep the paycheck coming. But upon investigation, you might find out that the ugly little plates go into the making of NASA rockets or the latest high-tech Internet devices. Learning this can turn meaningless drudgery into meaningful work and make a huge difference in your attitude toward your job. As your attitude changes and your work improves, others will take note.

Key Points

- Higher purpose is something (or things) that infuses life with joy and satisfaction, specifically because it lifts us up out of ourselves and connects us with others. When we have a higher purpose, we believe that we make a positive impact on the world.
- Research has shown that those who have a higher purpose— that is, who feel their lives are meaningful—tend to feel physically and mentally healthier than those who do not.
- Some people know what their higher purpose is when they are young; others do not. You can find your purpose in many ways including looking back over your life and seeing what has inspired you, what wrong you want to right, and so on.
- Having a higher purpose is good for business. Employees who tap into the leader's or company's higher purpose are more likely to be engaged with their work and to work harder and better.
- If you're a leader, imbuing your organization with your purpose can inspire the employees to work more enthusiastically and more carefully—which is good for them, for the world, and for your bottom line.

CHAPTER 8

Develop a Growth Mindset

Believe you can and you're halfway there.
—Theodore Roosevelt

llllllllllllllllllllllllllllllllllllllllllllllllllllll

Fashion designer Ralph Lauren came from a poor family yet wound up creating a worldwide multibillion-dollar fashion empire.

Jan Koum was fifteen when he and his mother came to the United States from Ukraine. Early on, he swept floors at a grocery store while his mother worked as a babysitter to earn money. Later, he taught himself the computer, dropped out of college, and went on to cofound WhatsApp.

The point of these brief stories is that where we begin doesn't have to dictate where we end up. More important than our starting position is believing that we can develop and learn and that we can master the skills necessary to move ahead. What's important is that we have a growth mindset, a conviction that we can and will continue to grow and learn until we reach our goal.

Ralph Lauren was a college dropout with no fashion training when he began designing men's ties. But he had a growth mindset as did Jan Koum. They believed they could learn what they needed to learn, develop the necessary skills, and plow ahead. And so they did.

P²D gives you tools to succeed, but these tools are not magic wands. You have to apply them. And you have to believe that you *can* reach your goals. Do you? Do you believe that you can learn what's required for you to move ahead and that you can develop the skills you may lack at the moment? Do you have a growth mindset?

Growth or Fixed Mindset?

Early on in life, I decided that I had absolutely no talent for softball. I tried it a few times, looked around and saw how much better everyone else was at it, and told myself to forget it. I convinced myself that I shouldn't bother trying again because I'd never be good at it.

That's an example of a fixed mindset. It comes from a belief that our talents are innate, that we're born with talent in some areas and no talent in others—and that's that. We can't get much better at what we're already good at doing because we were born that way. And we certainly won't get any better at what we're bad at doing. That's just the way it is.

You can see how the fixed mindset holds people back even when they're very young. Early in school, they decide they're no good at drawing or math, and they give up altogether. They strike out a few times in schoolyard baseball games and decide they are absolutely horrible. Or they are a slow runner and "know" there's no way they'll ever get faster. As adults, they bomb when they make a presentation at work and know they are bad and that there's no chance of getting ahead. It happened to me. After failing two parts of the CPA exam in 2007, I told myself that being a CPA just wasn't for me. I repeated this story over and over until I talked myself out of continuing to try. I never took that test again.

The opposite of the fixed mindset is the growth mindset. This is the belief that our talents are not fixed at birth and that we can continue growing, learning, and developing. I know of one seven-year-old boy who wanted to play Little League Baseball, but he kept striking out at bat and dropped almost every ball hit to him way out in the right field. Luckily, he had a growth mindset; and when baseball season ended, he spent an entire winter practicing. He begged his father and older brother to throw baseballs to him after school so he could learn to catch. He spent hours smacking stones with a baseball bat. He deliberately practiced hitting little stones because they were harder to hit than a full-sized baseball. The next summer, he was a Little League standout.

The difference between a growth mindset and a fixed mindset can be, and often is, the difference between success and failure. That's because the growth mindset tells you it's possible, so give it a try. You may fail, but you have the ability to come back again stronger and better prepared. The fixed mindset, on the other hand, tells you that you're only good at *A*, *B*, and *C*, so there's no point even trying *D* through *Z*. You close yourself off to most of the alphabet of opportunities.

Sometimes it's true that we lack the talent to shine in a certain area and are unlikely to develop it. After all, not everyone can earn a PhD in nuclear physics or win Olympic gold. But if we have a growth mindset, we'll give it a good try. We'll study up, look for mentors, seek opportunities, practice what needs to be practiced and take a flyer. We might even succeed the first time. Or the second, fifth, tenth, or fiftieth time! We might accomplish our goal all by ourselves. Or we might find someone who has the piece of knowledge or the skill we lack and succeed together. Or we might demonstrate such effort and devotion that someone invites us to join their team. Or we might realize that we can't make our original goal, but we can use the knowledge and skills we've developed to succeed in a different way.

But if we have a fixed mindset, we won't even try. We won't succeed with our original goal, we won't attract people to help us, we won't impress people who might hire us, and we won't succeed with our new goal. We'll stay right where we were, wondering why we can't seem to get ahead.

We all have a mix of mindsets, growth, and fixed. I know that from a young age, I had a fixed mindset about softball but was always certain that I could grow and learn when faced with the opportunity to immerse myself in the sport. And my decision on the spot at the seminar to change my business focus—from an accounting firm geared for small businesses to one specializing in government contracting—was a perfect example of the growth mindset. I didn't even know what all the obstacles might be when making the business switch, but I believed I could conquer them.

I don't want to mislead you; having a growth mindset is not a guarantee that you will be fabulously successful. But *not* having a growth mindset guarantees that you won't even come close.

Developing a Growth Mindset: Tips

The best thing you can do for the whole world is to make the most of yourself.

—Wallace Wattles

||||||||||||||||||||||||||||||||||||||||||||||||||||||||

Whether you have a growth mindset or a fixed mindset is a matter of nature and nurture of the interplay between your natural inclination and the way your parents, peers, schooling, and life experiences shaped your inclination. And while the "nature" part of your mindset may be fixed, the "nurture" need not be. You can shape it with your thoughts and actions.

Although there is no single best way to strengthen a growth mindset, there are helpful tips:

- **Understand that your life is about choices**—your life is not fixed and never has been. Yes, we're all born to certain circumstances with certain limitations. But you have the choice to stay where you are or to make a vigorous effort to move ahead.
- **Speak to yourself with a growth-mindset voice**—when you stumble, which you will do many times, remind yourself that all experiences in life have a lesson in them and that you're a beginner embarking on a long journey. When you stumble, don't say, "I failed." Instead, tell yourself, "I'm not yet there. But I've learned something from this stumble, and I am pushing ahead."
- **Prepare yourself well**—study, seek out advice and mentors, practice, and do whatever it takes to increase your knowledge and hone your skills. Every advance you make, no matter how small, is proof that you can grow.

- **Seek out opportunities to grow**—you can't grow unless you test yourself, so take on new and bigger challenges, like writing that first big report or making your first presentation. You might surprise yourself by succeeding the first time out. And if not, you'll learn where you are weak and know what you need to get better at.

- **Embrace criticism as an opportunity to grow**—criticism is not hurtful if you see it as an opportunity to learn. Yes, some people will offer criticism that's off base, irrelevant, or even mean. Ignore them and focus on the critiques that help you grow.

- **Don't worry about how you compare to others**—measuring yourself against others is a sure way to feel bad about yourself because you can always imagine that someone else is better than you in some way(s). Instead, think about where you were when you started and take pride in how far you've come.

- **Continually set new goals**—as soon as you've mastered *A*, move on to *B*, then to *C*, *D*, and the rest of the accomplishment alphabet. Never rest on your laurels, for you can be sure that your top competitors are not resting on theirs.

- **Take pride in the process, not the final result**—when you set an absolute final goal for yourself, you close off your growth mindset. After all, what's the point of growing beyond that arbitrary final goal? Instead, see yourself and your efforts as a lifelong work in progress—an endless opportunity to learn, grow, occasionally stumble, and always push forward.

Now, here are my personal favorite tips for developing a growth mindset. I stumbled across and used these tips even before I knew what a growth mindset was.

Developing a Growth Mindset: Rewrite Your Stories

It's never too late to be what we might have been.

—George Elliott

|||||||||||||||||||||||||||||||||||||||||||||||||||||||||

We all tell ourselves stories—long stories recounting every detail of things that have happened in the past and short stories that are really nothing more than statements such as "Every time I apply for a job, I get turned down." We also tell ourselves stories about the future, which we may call daydreams.

These stories are more than words floating around in our minds. They're more like "scripts" we play out in our lives. If our story is, "Every time I apply for a job, I get turned down," we will be reluctant to apply for jobs. We'll stick with the one we have rather than face more rejection. We'll wonder why we're so unworthy. Or maybe we know why we're unworthy and explain this with another story—this one blaming our parents, teachers, or life in general.

At their best, our stories help us sort things out and understand the world. They give us clarity. At their worst, our stories lock us in a figurative jail. That also gives us clarity, though of the wrong sort.

But we don't have to stick to our scripts—especially those that hold us back, that tell us we can't do it, or that life is against us for one reason or another. That's because we don't just *tell* ourselves stories—we also write them. And then we edit them over time.

As the writers and editors of our stories, we're perfectly free to change the contents of certain stories and just as free to toss out stories that hold us back so we can write new stories that take us forward. We can edit a story of some failure we had by adding to it: "But that was then before I learned …" or "I wasn't prepared nearly enough when it happened before, but I'm really prepared now." We can write a new chapter for the same story, continuing the narrative with a story about the future in which we talk about doing the same thing we failed at before—but this time doing it right because we're so well prepared. This time, succeeding and seeing how that success leads to more doors opening for us.

We can choose to discard or edit existing stories and write new ones in their place. We can choose to tell ourselves stories that help move us ahead, stories that talk about how we succeeded in the past through grit and determination by learning and becoming better at something. They may be stories from way back—of working hard at learning the multiplication tables or of mastering childhood piano lessons. They may be stories from more recent times or even stories of the future—stories of how we'll step out onto that stage and wow the audience with our speech, how we'll pass the test to get that certification or degree, or how we'll answer all the questions at the initial meeting with an important potential client.

We can't change our lives; we can't alter what has happened. But we can choose to see what happened through the lens of growth rather than of predetermined failure and tell ourselves new stories of how much we've grown since and how much more we will do so in the near future.

Our stories help us understand the world and, in so doing, tell us what we can and cannot do. Understand that the very first thing you should do—and you *can* do it—is to take ownership of your stories and edit or rewrite them such that they propel you toward your goal.

Developing a Growth Mindset: Show Up as if You've Already Made It

Extend your storytelling by putting yourself in the place of someone who has already turned the dream into reality and become that person. That is, act, talk, dress, and otherwise give everyone the impression that you've already made it.

I don't mean that you should try to fool people into believing you're something that you're not. That only works for a little while at best. I mean that you should look, speak, think, and behave as if you are already the person you want to be. From an early age, my youngest son was interested in the medical field. He excelled in math and science and loved to play with stethoscopes. When it was time to apply for college, he had one school on his list. He applied and was accepted for early admission to an Ivy League university to begin his collegiate studies toward a career in the medical field. He had interned at a hospital in high school, rising to the position of a lead volunteer by the time he was a senior, organizing the other students' schedules and assignments. At the time, he didn't realize that his P^{2}D for a career in the medical field guided his growth mindset to walk a path toward his purpose and destiny.

Stories like this demonstrate that showing up as if you have already made it does two things. First, it reinforces your belief in yourself. Second, it invites others to listen to your story. If you want to be a leader, for example, be seen as a leader. Don't shirk responsibility and don't try to get others to make decisions or otherwise act like a follower. Learn about the different leadership styles and know which are appropriate and when. Everywhere you go, behave as a leader would even if you're not yet the leader you want to be. This means that you have to learn how a leader behaves at work, in meetings with peers, when reporting to superiors, when dealing with subordinates, when soliciting the opinions of advisors, and so on. You have to understand how to be seen as a leader in every possible situation because you never know when you'll have an opportunity to display your leadership qualities.

Showing up as if you have already made it is a way of constantly telling yourself that you can be successful. And when others respond positively, you'll be able to write a new story about how others see you as a leader.

You may want to consider investing in a leadership coach to ensure that you are behaving, dressing, and otherwise being the person you want to become. It may be unfair, but the reality is that appearance and presentation matter. Grooming matters as do speech and behavior. Even the way you eat your soup can matter—and it would be a shame to learn that you lost the leadership position over that!

A leadership coach helps you align your appearance, communication, behavior, and more with what you want to be. This can include everything from designing your wardrobe and going shopping with you to training you for proper etiquette. If you work with a leadership coach, remember that the point is not to fool people. It's to bring out the qualities in you that make others feel as if you really are that leader you want to be or whatever else it is that you are aiming for.

No matter what it is you're striving for, show up as if you already have it. When you go to a job interview, for example, show up as if you already have that job. Study up on the position, the necessary skills, company, industry, and everything else that matters; dress, walk, and talk the part and let the people interviewing you see you as the person they're looking for. Show up as if you've already made it to the final destination (see chapter 3 for more on branding).

Developing a Growth Mindset: Behave As If Someone Is Always Watching

There should never be a moment when you do not speak, act, and otherwise behave as the person you want to be—as the person living your higher destiny. Always carry yourself as if someone is watching, for you never know when someone will be attracted to your shining star and become your sponsor, advocate, mentor, or door opener or otherwise put you into situations that carry you closer to your destination. You never know when a new opportunity to grow or to shine will appear.

Even if you're not entirely happy in your current situation or feel you will not reach your destiny, behave as if someone is always watching.

A young immigrant named Sidney Poitier always behaved as if someone was watching—because they were. He auditioned before casting directors who could be abrupt and cruel, and he acted for directors and producers who could be very demanding—all this under the harsh glare of the open racism that pervaded the United States in the 1940s and 1950s when he was beginning his career as an actor.

He was not an instant success. When Poitier auditioned at New York City's American Negro Theatre, his heavy Caribbean accent annoyed the director, who suggested that he give up acting and look for a job as a dishwasher. Instead, Poitier worked hard to master the American accent and continued improving his acting skills; soon enough, he was accepted at the same American Negro Theatre that had rejected him so cruelly. By the late 1950s, he was a major movie star, appearing over the course of a storied career in films such as *A Raisin in the Sun*; *Guess Who's Coming to Dinner*; *To Sir, with Love*; and *Lilies of the Field*, for which he won an Oscar for Best Actor.

I can't guarantee that you'll go from dishwashing to the Oscars, but I can tell you that people notice what you do. That's why it's vital that you always act as if someone is watching. It only takes one person to open that door, make that recommendation, or arrange that introduction that changes your life.

Developing a Growth Mindset: Let Your Light Shine

In my decades as a soldier and businesswoman, I've been struck by the number of people who seem to fear being noticed. They take backseats and never speak up at meetings, let others take credit for their ideas or work, and otherwise fail to let their light shine. In fact, they seem to want to dim their light lest they be noticed. Some seem to be shy or fear being labeled aggressive or too pushy. Sometimes it's excessive modesty that holds people back, while other times there may be cultural factors involved.

If you are deliberately pulling the shade down over your light, you are all but guaranteeing that you will not be noticed, supported, endorsed, promoted, put on a team, given financial backing, or otherwise given the support you need—and deserve.

Shyness holds many people back. I've seen people shaking as they step up to present in a meeting, speaking so softly they can barely be heard, and staring down at the table rather than looking at the audience.

If shyness is holding you back, set aside the idea that you're either a brilliant conversationalist/speaker or a terrible one. Remind yourself that becoming comfortable in business settings, networking sessions, and personal interactions is a journey and that every time you show up and speak up—even a little—you've taken another step forward. Also, keep reminding yourself that you have something to contribute. You know something, or you can do something that will help others. They are dying to meet and work with you, and both you and they will benefit if you speak up.

If fear is holding you back, remind yourself that you are very good at what you do. You've prepared yourself; you've mastered the knowledge or skills. You can perform at a very high level. And if you miss the mark or make a mistake, congratulations! Every successful person and everyone who has mastered their destiny has made plenty of mistakes, some of them very embarrassing. Now that you've made a mistake and humiliated yourself or tossed away lots of money, you're just like them.

Developing a Growth Mindset: Work, Work, Work!

Serial entrepreneur Mark Cuban, the billionaire owner of the Dallas Mavericks basketball team, has invested in numerous companies over the years. Some of his investments have been successful; others have not. But he has said, "The best investment I ever made was investing in myself, first and foremost."[24] How did he invest in himself? By working hard to master the knowledge required to get ahead.

Soon after completing his studies in business at the University of Indiana, Cuban moved to Dallas where he worked as a bartender and later found employment at Your Business Software, selling personal computer software. Often broke, he ran up so much credit card debt that his cards were cut. He slept on the floor of an apartment he shared with six others and sometimes couldn't afford to pay the utility bill, which meant that the apartment didn't always have electricity.

Cuban didn't have money, but he did have a tremendous willingness to work—specifically, to work at learning. Night after night, he pored through software manuals he had brought home from the store, studying Lotus, dBase, and other systems. No matter how late it was when he got home, he studied. Also, while at the store, he made it a point to learn how to install the different types of software, as well as to configure and run them.

Doing this was "painfully time consuming,"[25] Cuban has said, but it helped him earn a reputation as an expert and earn more money in sales commissions. It also prepared him to found a new company when he was fired from his sales job. The new business, MicroSolutions, turned a struggling salesman into a millionaire and launched him on the path to becoming a billionaire.

If you want to move ahead, whether as an employee or an entrepreneur, you'll have to make major investments of time, resources, and effort. And through it all, expect to work, work, and

---

[24] Taylor Locke, "Mark Cuban on the 'best investment' he every made: 'Most people don't put in the time' to do it." *CNBC MakeIt* (October 5, 2020), accessed January 4, 2022, https://www.cnbc.com/2020/10/05/mark-cuban-this-is-the-best-investment-i-ever-made.html.
[25] Ibid.

work some more. Becoming a leader is hard work, but if being a leader is truly your destiny, you'll find that you can do the work. You may be tired, you may wonder where it is all heading, but you'll be able to do what it takes to become the leader you were meant to be.

Living the Growth Mindset

Nothing is worse than looking back over your life, sighing, and saying, "If only." To avoid that unhappy fate, focus on developing a growth mindset.

You have the passion, perseverance, and drive. You have a higher purpose, and you have the tools and talents necessary to plow ahead. Add in a generous serving of growth mindset, and your success is all but inevitable.

Key Points

- Where we started in life doesn't have to determine where we end up if we have a growth mindset.
- The growth mindset tells us that no matter where we are now, we can continually learn and grow and push ahead toward our goal.
- We all have a growth mindset to one degree or another. We can strengthen our growth mindset by choosing to do so and then pursuing that choice with unflagging determination.
- We can strengthen our growth mindset even more by showing up as if we have already made it; behaving as if someone is always watching; letting our light shine; and being willing to work, work, and work some more.
- There is no easy path to success. But developing a powerful growth mindset guarantees that you'll remain on the path to success—no matter how many times you stumble—and that you'll continually progress toward your goal.

CHAPTER 9

Claim Your Destiny

It takes courage to grow up and become who you really are.

—E. E. Cummings

||||||||||||||||||||||||||||||||||||||||||||||||||||

Ursula Burns was raised by her mother in a New York housing project. Mom made ends meet by running a daycare center in their home and taking on cleaning jobs. Despite her poor upbringing, Ursula became CEO of Xerox in 2009, making her the first African American woman to head up a Fortune 500 company. She held that position for seven years and then served another seven as chairman of Xerox.

Kat Cole's father separated from the family when she was nine. Mom, raising Kat and her two sisters on her own, sometimes had to feed the family for $10 a week. Kat began working when she was fifteen and became a hostess at a Hooters restaurant at age seventeen. She began climbing the ladder, becoming vice president of Hooters, then president of Cinnabon, and then COO and president of Focus Brands—which owns Cinnabon and other well-known food franchises.

There are many more stories like this—too many to count, let alone recount. The details differ from story to story, but the point is always the same: where we started in life doesn't have to be where we end up. We can claim our destiny, a destiny that we and we alone determine, a destiny filled with hope and progress.

We aren't born with magical stardust in our pockets; there are no guarantees in life. Even if we are born to rich and powerful parents, there's no telling if we will live lives of purpose and meaning or of disappointment and despair. This means that if you want a life of meaning and purpose and if you want to reach your goals, you have to go out and make it happen. And as many people who have gone before have shown, it can be done!

The P²D-Driven Life

Great works are performed, not by strength, but by perseverance.

—Samuel Johnson

||||||||||||||||||||||||||||||||||||||||||||||||||||

Claiming your destiny may not be easy. You will face endless obstacles, doubters will tell you to give it up, and your fears will hold you back. But it can be done if you tap into your passion, perseverance, and drive—and tie that to a growth mindset.

Many people have great dreams. Many have great ideas that could make them successful and perhaps even change the world. But a dream or idea that just sits there on the couch next to you will never come to fruition. It takes passion to turn a thought into action, perseverance to keep going over the long haul and drive to continue racing ahead even when you are exhausted and have no roadmap to success.

Too many of us lead lives lacking a purpose, staying power, and determination. This is a shame, for to succeed in our complex world, we must live a life defined by P²D. The P²D-defined life is about making choices—choices that remove the distractions from life and allow us to focus on our goals. Most of the choices we need to make will be obvious and easy: Do we really need to spend all those hours on social media? Or spend all that money to buy a fancy car when a less expensive one will do? Other choices will be harder to make. We may enjoy spending extra time with our friends and really want to see all our kids' school plays and other events. But when we hesitate to make the hard choices, we're threatening our P²D. At this point, we must choose to rev up our P²D to create the life we want to live.

We can make the necessary choices when we have a burning passion to achieve our goals. That passion will fuel our perseverance and drive and carry us into building our brand. Our brand is the "story" that sets us apart from all others. It's the story that tells customers, employees, partners, bankers, and others why we are worth buying from, working for, working with, and supporting. When our passion for what we are doing is strong, our brand will shine and ring true—because it is genuine—and others will be powerfully attracted to us.

And we need other people—plenty of them. We need a network of people who can help us by offering referrals, giving us advice, buying from us, serving as partners, and more. When we know and are passionate about our purpose and are willing to make the necessary choices to achieve it, we can easily assemble a powerful network filled with resources and opportunities. Of course, we must remember that a network is made up of both a net and a lot of work, and then do all that work. This will be much easier to do when we are passionate about what we are doing, willing to persevere, and driven to succeed. Others will pick up on the flame of our P^2D and be attracted to us.

We'll find that it is much easier to keep our P^2D burning bright when we are intentional, when our actions align with our words, and when everything we do is designed to carry us closer to our goal. It's easy to be unintentional and to waste our energy on unproductive actions and on people who pull us away from our goal. Tapping into our P^2D helps us guard our time, continuously improve, push past errors, ask for help, and otherwise forge ahead. It becomes a virtuous cycle, with P^2D helping us to remain very intentional—our lives of intentionality fanning the flames of our P^2D and on and on. We become an unstoppable force, sweeping obstacles aside as we sprint toward the goal.

We must also sweep aside our fears or at least learn to control and use them. Many of us allow our fears to sabotage our P^2D, and we find ourselves feeling defeated, wondering why nothing seems to work out for us. The human brain is a wonderful fear-generating machine, which is why fear is likely to derail us unless we are passionate and driven to succeed, willing to persevere no matter what it takes.

We've made our choices, developed a strong personal brand, and created a powerful network; we've learned to become intentional about everything we do and set aside our fears. Now we must find our higher purpose in life if we haven't already. This is vital, for having a higher purpose fuels the flame of our P²D, making work a pleasure; failure an opportunity to learn; and obstacles a chance to grow stronger, more clever, and more resilient. Having a higher purpose makes life meaningful and pleasurable, which means that success is all but guaranteed—no matter how we define success.

Finally, we must make sure that our P²D and all the tools associated with it are linked to a growth mindset and to the belief that we can and will succeed.

Live the P²D Life

Always remember that you can live the P²D-driven life, and you can claim your destiny. Your destiny does not have to include earning a billion dollars or being famous or powerful. Perhaps your destiny is to run a small business in a neighborhood that desperately needs your products or to work at a job just to earn enough money to devote the rest of your life to some great endeavor.

However, you define your destiny, it can be yours if you live the P²D-defined life. And no matter what the circumstances of your birth or family of origin or educational or financial status, you can choose to tap into and build your passion, perseverance, and drive—and to succeed!